3.T
vision

TRUTH TRIUMPHS OVER TRAGEDY

FOCUSING ON GOD'S WORD
IN THE MIDST OF THE STORM

LIZ MORELAND

TRUTH TRIUMPHS OVER TRAGEDY

FOCUSING ON GOD'S WORD
IN THE MIDST OF THE STORM

Tate Publishing & Enterprises

Published by Tate Publishing & Enterprises, LLC

127 E. Trade Center Terrace | Mustang, Oklahoma 73064 USA

1.888.361.9473 | www.tatepublishing.com

Tate Publishing is committed to excellence in the publishing industry. The company reflects the philosophy established by the founders, based on Psalms 68:11,
"The Lord gave the word and great was the company of those who published it."

Book design copyright © 2007 by Tate Publishing, LLC. All rights reserved.
Cover design by Elizabeth A. Mason
Interior design by Jacob Crissup

Published in the United States of America

ISBN: 978-1-6024714-2-9
07.08.22

Dedication

This book is primarily dedicated to the Father, Son and Holy Spirit from whom all blessings flow. *3T Vision* would not have been realized without your grace and mercy.

I also dedicate this book to my family who sacrificed so that I could fulfill God's calling on my life. I love you.

And a special note to my son, Jake: Mommy loves you "to the moon and back, and around and around the sun."

Acknowledgements

First and foremost I want to thank our heavenly Father, His Son, and the Holy Spirit whose guidance, protection and anointing made this book a reality. And to Christ Jesus, I thank you for carrying me every step of the way through the storms that have plagued my life. I know there is only one set of footprints in the sand covering the last six years, carrying me to the point where I could fulfill God's calling.

To the women who so graciously volunteered their time and powerful testimonies of what it means to have 3T Vision: I can never thank you enough. Your stories will refresh, bless and inspire every heart and soul that reads them.

I will forever be grateful to my husband, Larry, for supporting me in this endeavor. His prayers and encouragement were invaluable. I thank my precious little boy, Jake, for understanding when Mommy couldn't always spend the time with him that she wanted to. As long as he knew that Mommy was "working for God," he was okay with that.

How can you ever thank that person who led you to the Lord? Julie, I will always love you.

Thanks go out to my mother-in-law and my niece, especially in the latter stages of the project, for helping out and allowing me to put some extra time into the project. God always has a way of working things out for our good and His glory (Romans 8:28).

To mom and dad and the rest of my family in Toronto, Canada:

Thank you for understanding that I couldn't always be with you while I was committed to this project. Please know that I *am always* with you in spirit and prayer.

Special acknowledgements to Karen and Bonny who not only volunteered their stories, they also acted as my "second set of eyes;" critiquing the stories before I sent them in to be edited. Thank you for finding the time and energy in your already overcommitted lives.

To all of my friends and family who put up with me as I neared my deadline; I appreciate everyone's prayers, support and understanding.

We all have that one true friend who loves us despite all of our pimples and warts; who completely understands, encourages, lifts us up, and prays for us continually. Delana, you are that friend in my life. Thank you for always being there, especially as I undertook this endeavor.

Thank you, Pastor Michael Abernathy and Miss Shirley, and Christy and James McDonald for your ever-present mentorship and example of "who I want to be when I grow up;" particularly as I mature in my walk with the Lord. And to my precious church family, your constant prayers and encouragement meant more to me than you'll ever know.

Finally, I would like to thank Tate Publishing for their faith in me as a first-time author. I would particularly like to thank Dr. Richard Tate, founder of Tate Enterprises, LLC, for his empathy and understanding during the season of strife my family experienced as I worked to complete *3T Vision*. He is a faith-filled, professional "class act," as is the entire Publishing house. Special acknowledgements go out to Jesika Lay in Submissions and Dave Dolphin, Director of Production. I'd also like to thank my Conceptual Editor, Allison Johnson, and Graphics Designer, Liz Mason, for their professionalism and words of encouragement.

Table of Contents

Your eye is the lamp of your body. When your eyes are good, your whole body also is full of light. But when they are bad, your body also is full of darkness. See to it then, that the light within you is not darkness.

Luke 11:34–35, NIV

When Jesus spoke again to the people, he said, "I am the light of the world. Whoever follows me will never walk in darkness, but will have the light of life."

John 8:12, NIV

Introduction

3T Vision: Truth Triumphs over Tragedy. In other words, if we rely on God's word, He can carry us through the darkness and on to victory. It sounds simple enough doesn't it? But how often do we rely on ourselves or others, or wallow in self pity when a season of tragedy befalls us? Why do we need to be clobbered over the head, brought to our knees, before we finally look up and cry out to our merciful Father for help?

Until about six years ago, I was one of those stubborn, self-reliant, spiritually skeptical women of the World. But by God's grace and mercy, I've lived the *Vision* up close and personal. I couldn't have written this book otherwise—I wouldn't have had the right to. But the Lord has called me to use the talents He has blessed me with to reach out to others. He gave me the term and the concept of *3T Vision* one day as I was praying and searching my heart for a way to serve Him and others. It had been four and a half years since I had dedicated my life to Jesus Christ; vowing to use my God-given talents from that day on, to testify about His love, grace and mercy.

3T Vision then has been born not only out of a desire to reach out to those in need of encouragement, but first and foremost, it is meant to glorify our Lord and Savior, Jesus Christ. To know Christ is to know that He *is* the way, the truth and the life (John 14: 6(2), KJV). He has so graciously and mercifully provided His truth so that we might reach out, grasp it, and triumph over the tragedies that come our way.

For as all Christians know, Satan will and does attack. But there is power in the blood and there is power in the Word.

> Finally, my brethren, be strong in the Lord, and in the power of his might. Put on the whole armor of God, that ye may be able to stand against the wiles of the devil.
>
> Ephesians 6:10, 11, KJV

Our Lord has provided us with the weapons we need to combat and defeat the enemy. The Bible is the Christian's arsenal. And hallelujah! Truth always triumphs over tragedy!

But there is also a crucial, pivotal moment that bridges the gap between our tragedy and the application of truth to that tragedy. We cannot expect to emerge triumphant until we make that *choice* that will forever change our lives and either begin or renew our walk with Jesus Christ. We have to *choose* to turn our lives over to Him when our lives are turned upside down, when our path begins to twist and turn in ways we could have never imagined. It is at this point that we need to turn everything over to Him and *choose* to:

> Trust in the Lord with all [our] heart; and lean not on [our] own understanding. In all [our] ways acknowledge him, and he shall direct [our] path.
>
> Proverbs 3:5–6, KJV

For where would be today, had the key women in the Bible not followed this course? Today's believers are the benefactors of their victories!

Let's take a look at the Book of Ruth for a moment. What if Ruth had not remained faithful to God and loyal to her mother-in-law, Naomi? Sacrificing her own security, she demonstrated love and respect for her mother-in-law, when she followed her back to Bethlehem after they were both widowed.

Ruth could have taken the easy way out. She could have remained in Moab as did her widowed sister-in-law. She had every Worldly right to. As a widowed Moabite woman, Ruth would face a life of hardship living in Bethlehem. Both women would live in poverty as widows, but Ruth would also be a minority outcast.

In addition, both women decided to honor God's laws during a dark time in which Israel's people were rebelling. In the midst of their tragedy, both women remained open and obedient to God. The result was a marriage between Ruth and an equally obedient, Godly man named Boaz. God poured out his grace and mercy, blessing their union with the bloodline of David...and eventually Christ Jesus!

Fast forward 1200 years to the story of Mary and Elisabeth: two courageous women, direct descendants of David, who chose to obey God despite the personal sacrifices they would have to make (Luke 1:1–4:13). Mary chose to believe and accept the angel, Gabriel's, message that she would bare the Messiah. Imagine the responsibility and risk involved in that proposition: the unwed thirteen-year-old virgin was accepting a calling on her life that would subject her to severe punishment and rejection (not exactly the most ideal of circumstances in the Hebrew culture during that time period). Imagine the amount of faith she must have had to take on the extraordinary vision that God had for her!

Her much older and very wise cousin, Elisabeth's reaction was one of support, joy and confirmation. She too had recently become pregnant with a son after Gabriel paid a visit to her husband, Zechariah. Gabriel also instructed the couple to name their son John, and informed them that John would eventually baptize the Messiah. They, too, obeyed God, despite the possible repercussions.

The enormity of the responsibility these women were given is almost unfathomable. Both women knew they could face extreme persecution from the Pharisees who were desperately trying to hold on to their power despite the Roman occupation. Either woman could have cowered away from such a sacrifice. Instead, both women *rejoiced* in the gifts God had given them! They were secure in their knowledge that if they obeyed God, if they remained true to the vision put before them, He would deliver them from what could have been utter tragedy. They did, and He did, and Elisabeth and Mary, gave birth to John the Baptist and Jesus Christ, respectively!

The point is that all of God's miracles in the midst of tragedy beg the question: how can my 3T Vision affect the generations to come? The word Vision plays a dual role in the concept of what it means to have 3T Vision. First, it means that we must *focus* on the *truth* in order to get through life's trials and tribulations. But secondly, it also relates to the belief that God has a predestined vision for our lives. Often-times when we begin to pursue that mission, the enemy will try to deter us. But as long as we focus on the truth, we can fulfill the mission, despite any tragedy that comes our way.

The following scriptures tie these two principles together:

> ...If ye continue in my word, then are ye my disciples indeed; And ye shall know the truth, and the truth shall make you free.
>
> John 8:32, KJV

> Where there is no vision, the people perish...but whoso putteth his trust in the Lord shall be safe.
>
> Proverbs 29:18–25, KJV

The inspirational stories you are about to read follow several ordinary women who fought back against an incredible darkness. At some point they *chose* to use Christ's Truth. They unknowingly *chose* to put on *3T Vision* glasses and were rewarded with triumph over their personal tragedy. They personify the Biblical over-comer.

My prayer for you as you share their stories is that you will:

- begin to develop your own *3T Vision;* a mechanism you can rely on when coping with life's difficulties

- find comfort in knowing that you are not alone in your trials

- deepen your relationship with the Lord and learn to rely on His truth despite the circumstances

You may be in the middle of your own storm right now, fighting off the "fiery darts of the wicked" (Eph. 6:16, KJV). To get the most out of this reading experience, I encourage you to actively participate in an experience of spiritual growth. That's why *3T Vision* is rife with scriptural references and an entire page at the end of each chapter has been provided for you to record your reflections.

Because, in reality we're all just one moment, one phone call or one medical test away from tragedy. So we need to be prepared. We need to build the fortress *before* the storm. Won't it be comforting to know that you'll have Christ's Truth and a little *3T Vision* to get you through the fire?

May God bless you and keep you in His infinite care as you embark on the spiritual journey before you.

Note: Many of the names in each story have been changed to protect confidentiality.

Chapter 1

The Author's Story
Putting the Vision Where My Mouth Is

"I believe that every survivor, whatever the tragedy, is given a precious gift: the gift of clarity. In an instant, our priorities, our purpose, our faith is clarified in a way that we may have never known, or appreciated, had we not had to walk through the fire. I praise God for this blessing and for his ever-present love and support."

Liz Moreland—breast cancer survivor

"I shall not die, but live, and declare the works of the Lord."

Psalms 118:17, KJV

"Happy birthday to you, happy birthday to you..."

"Mom, stop," I quietly interrupted.

"Happy birthday dear Liz..."

"Mom! Please! Stop!" I insist, louder this time, my voice beginning to crack with emotion.

"What, Liz? What is it?" Her sing-song voice shifts to panic mode.

There's no other way to say it, so I just say it: "I have breast cancer, Mom."

In the Blink of an Eye

It was June 26, 2001, my thirty-fourth birthday. I had received the devastating news from the breast care specialist the day before. The cruel twist was in the timing of the diagnosis. I wasn't going to have time to process the shock of it all before having to talk to friends and family. They were all going to call me on my birthday and I was going to have to give them an unexpected slap in the face.

And the worst aspect of that phase was telling my parents. No parent should have to hear that from their child. And no adult child wants to burden their parents with that kind of devastating news. In fact, if I could have gotten through the whole experience without telling them, I would have. Living 1,000 miles apart (I live in North Georgia and my parents live in Canada), didn't help matters either. There are moments in life, when, no matter how old you are, you just ache for your mom and dad to hold you, to tell you everything's going to be all right. This was one of those times.

The parental hugs would have to wait and a fact was a fact: I had breast cancer—and not just any breast cancer. I had been diagnosed with the rarest (accounting for just one percent of all breast cancer diagnosis), most aggressive and most deadly form: inflammatory, infiltrating, stage III carcinoma. This type of cancer sneaks up on you out of no where, then grows and spreads like wildfire.

I had been misdiagnosed for three weeks with acute mastitis. All of the doctors insisted I was too young and the tumor had grown too quickly. When the final diagnosis came, the tumor was 10 cm. That's about the size of a tennis ball! To give you a little perspective, a tumor of 2.5 cm is what catapults a patient from stage II to stage III, and puts you at a higher risk of the tumor spreading to other areas of the body (metastasizing).

Needless to say, this unexpected turn of events had thrown my family's life into the uncharted wilderness of cancer jargon. We were hearing and using words we never thought would pertain to one of us. It was as if one moment I was a healthy, active wife to Larry and mother to Jake (then fourteen months old), and the next thing I knew I was a cancer patient. In the blink of an eye, I was taking CT and bone scans; preparing for a nine-month regimen of chemotherapy, surgery, and radiation followed by a second round of chemo. I could think of about a thousand better ways to spend nine months!

Taking Baby Steps: Seeking Jesus

But this story really began in April of that same year. Raised in a non-religious atmosphere (I can count on one hand the number of times I attended church with my mother as a child) I had been taking baby steps toward a relationship with God for years.

However, I had never been able to wrap my brain around what I referred to as "the Jesus thing." Who was he *really?* Was he really the Son of God or a well-meaning prophet who just truly believed he was the Son of God? And what was his purpose? Why did so many people vehemently believe in him while others railed against the very suggestion of a human form of God and his seemingly impossible resurrection?

What was it all about? I believed in God and being the best possible person I could be. I believed in the Golden Rule: treating others as I wanted to be treated. But I didn't believe that I needed to go to church, and was turned off by the constant talk of money related to organized religion.

All of this began to change in the late summer of 2000 (allow me to digress even further for just a moment) when I began a friendship with a neighbor of mine, Julie. In His infinite wisdom, the Lord knew what was coming and provided me with an awesome spiritual mentor, a woman after God's own heart. Julie invited me to attend her Pentecostal church and ladies Bible study. She pursued me, determined to lead me to the Lord. I attended several services and a Bible study meeting, but ultimately, I was still sitting on my lazy spiritual duff. For Christmas that year, Larry gave me a beautiful study Bible.

The Proverbial Kick in the Pants

But on that beautiful spring day in April, 2001 as I pushed my son in his stroller, I found myself talking to God. In actuality, I was making a confession and a request that would change my life, and those around me, forever. "God, I don't appreciate my life. I have a husband who loves me, a healthy, beautiful baby boy, a beautiful home, supportive family members and wonderful friends, yet I'm still self-destructive."

At this point I need to explain the nature of my self-destructive tendencies. I was on the cusp of developing a drinking problem. There was a history of alcoholism in my family and up until the age of 33, I had kept this demon at bay. But the craving for a drink at the end of a hectic day was becoming a daily occurrence. Every time I went to the grocery store, I tried to talk myself out of going down "that aisle."

"I'm not going to go down that aisle...I'm not going down that aisle..." Then as the wheels on the cart made that fateful turn, that little voice would say, "I'm going down the aisle...I deserve a relaxing drink at the end of my day. It's not a big deal."

But that's how the enemy works, whispering little rationalizations...no, lies...into your ear; lies that keep you from developing to your full potential, from developing a relationship with Christ. And I was falling for that slow erosion of my values. In *Battlefield of the Mind:* [1] *Devotional,* Joyce Meyer describes the process as Satan's construction of "well-laid plans."

> [Satan] moves slowly and cautiously (after all, well-laid plans take time)....The enemy of our mind starts out with little things–little dissatisfactions, small desires–and builds from there...That's how Satan works—slowly, diligently, and in small ways. Rarely does he approach us through direct assault or frontal attacks. All Satan needs is an opening—an opportunity to inject unholy, self-centered thoughts into our heads. If we don't kick them back out they stay inside. And he can continue his evil, destructive plan.* (5–6)

What Satan hadn't counted on, was the fact that my heart's one true desire was to be a good, nurturing mother. He didn't count on the fact that that desire was stronger than my craving for that drink at the end of the day. He didn't count on the fact that my conscience would override his lies and that I would eventually reach out to God to resolve that conflict.

Because by this time, that one glass of wine while preparing dinner had turned into three or four drinks a night! When I finally realized how many drinks I was consuming in a week, I was shocked.

My conversation with God while pushing Jake in the stroller that day continued, "I've been stubborn and self-destructive my whole life, Lord. Despite all the success I've had, all the blessings in my life, I always manage to destroy it on some level. I can't believe the alcoholic monster is catching up with me. I need your help, God, but I've been lazy in my pursuit of you. I have so much. My life is so rich, but I don't feel the richness. I want to appreciate my life in a deeper way but I don't know how. As with everything else, I know it's going to take a good swift kick in the pants to straighten me out."

I had no idea what I was asking for. But God did. And He had more than just a kick in the pants in store for me. He was about to allow me to bring myself to my knees through my destructive behavior—to that all familiar place where all we can do is look up.

And those little baby steps I had been taking? Well, I was about to run to God in leaps and bounds…in fact, I would feel like a human rocket, traveling through my spiritual journey at the speed of light.

Looking back now, I compare this cry for help to David's cry to the Lord as he fled from Saul, living alone in the wilderness. My wilderness consisted of my barren, unsaved soul. The enemy was in hot pursuit with the fleshly temptation of alcohol. He had a foothold in my life and he was filling my head with lies; "seeking to steal, kill and destroy" (John 10:10). The enemy had told me all of my life, that I didn't deserve good things, and that there was no point in hoping for good things because I would always be disappointed.

But today was different. Today I knew that I wanted more. Today I made the choice to turn to God. And Satan was not a happy camper. Not six weeks after my "tête-à-tête" with the Lord, I received the diagnosis of cancer.

The Choice

But again I was faced with a choice: I could become bitter and harden my heart, angry with God for "allowing" this to happen to me, or I could turn toward him and search out His truth in my time of tragedy. I know that I'm here today because I chose the latter.

I'm not going to lie to you. The first few days I was in shock, frozen with fear. Of course my main fear was that I might not be around to raise my fourteen-month-old son; that Jake could lose his mother at a very tender age. He may not remember me. He may never know how much his mother loved him.

Over and over my father's words of encouragement played in my head, "Liz, you've never lost at anything in your entire life. You're not going to lose at this either." But I instinctively knew that I was in over my head on this one.

True to His character, the Lord placed all of the right people in my path. People I didn't even know including a pastor and women from a nearby church visited my home and prayed for me and my family. Friends and family members from near and far leant their prayers and support.

Dealing with health issues of his own at the time, my father supported me from a distance with daily phone calls. My mother was able to make a couple of visits to help out, which I greatly appreciated.

Julie came over and prayed with me during the moments I felt like I was going to crawl out of my skin. She gave me index cards full of relevant scripture that I meditated on continuously. On those cards were jewels of God's wisdom regarding illness, fear, anxiety, worry and hope for the future. Perhaps most importantly she referred me to 1 John so that I would come to know the awesome depth of God's love for man. The words were comforting, but I was still struggling with paralyzing fear and brief panic attacks.

On the third day, I decided I couldn't go on in that mode. I prayed, "Lord, you are in control of this situation. There is no way around this predicament. I'm used to being able to figure my way out of any situation. But there is no way around this. I can't get through this without you Lord."

At that moment of prayer, I felt a wave of revelation come over me. For the first time in my life, I felt close to God. For the first time, I was praying in the spirit: "God, I'm not going to fear this situation. Instead, I'm going to embrace it as a journey–and I accept this journey as long as I have you to walk through the fire with me. All I ask is that you give me the courage, strength and peace that I'll need to get up every day and look after my little boy. He shouldn't have to suffer because of what I'm about to go through."

And, as always, the good Lord delivered on his promise:

> Ask and it shall be given unto you; seek and ye shall find; knock, and
> the door shall be opened unto you...
>
> Matthew 7:7

I awoke the next morning with the "peace of God, which passeth understanding" (Philippians 4:7). I now had the strength and the courage to face the enemy head on.

Later that morning, I ran into Julie outside on the street. We were both checking our mailboxes at the same time. She came running across the street.

"Liz!" she said excitedly. "At three o'clock this morning, I was laying awake in bed praying for you, crying out to God in frustration. I asked him what I needed to do for you, what was it I needed to pray for you. And he told me to get on my face on the floor and pray for the peace you needed. And so I did."

"Julie," I said, goose bumps rising and chills racing down my spine. "I've got it! I have the peace and the strength! I prayed for it last night too!"

Caught up in the emotion of the moment, we hugged and began to cry.

My Christian mentor put me at arms length and said, "Liz, I can see it. I can see it in your countenance. You've got it! You've really got it!"

Sweet Surrender

I went on to my appointments. Everything was moving so fast. I was diagnosed on the Tuesday and, because of the nature of my cancer, my oncologist scheduled all the scans and tests necessary to begin my first chemo treatment on the Friday! These tests would show whether or not the disease had spread and would determine the course of my treatment. I carried and read my Bible and Bruce Wilkinson's best seller, *The Prayer of Jabez* to every test. Wilkinson's book made so much sense to me. Between the Scriptures about healing, First and Second John and *The Prayer of Jabez,* I was finally able to understand God's love for me. I prayed and read and cried and prayed some more.

Still waiting on some of the test results, I sat in a courtyard in between chemo treatments. It was lunch time and Larry and Jake had gone to the cafeteria to get me something to eat. Again, I spoke to God: "Lord, regardless of the test results, whether or not the cancer has metastasized, I place my trust in you. I will be okay either way because I know you're with me." At that moment I felt warmth that I had never felt before; like a warm blanket, comforting me, giving me a sense of peace I had never felt.

During another doctor visit, my cell phone rang. It was the oncologist's assistant. She could barely contain her excitement, "Liz! The scans are clean! [The cancer] hasn't gone anywhere else!"

"Praise God!" was all I could say before I melted into tears on the examining table. I knew that God had rewarded me for my unconditional faith. And I believe that that moment in the courtyard was the moment I received salvation as well as the Holy Spirit. I cried for joy continuously for hours after that and then on and off for the rest of the day.

My first call was to Julie. Through the tears, I said, "Julie! Today is my first day as a child of God!"

"Happy birthday, Liz," she said. "Today is your second birthday! You've just been born again!" It was June 29th, 2001. We continued to cry joyful tears together, all the while praising Jesus and the Father.

From that moment in the courtyard on, my whole perspective and approach to life changed. The supernatural experience is almost impossible to put into words. The best way I can describe it is that I felt like a babe swaddled in the warmth of a blanket of love; a love that only Jesus can provide. There was no fear, only peace.

How arrogant I'd been to assume that I was the only one capable of raising my son. Ultimately, Jake was God's child on loan to me.

Regardless of what would happen to me, God would provide for Jake. Once this fear was lifted, I was free.

I called mom that night, and before I could even begin my testimony, she jumped in and asked, "What happened to you this afternoon between 1:30 and 2:00?"

I couldn't believe it. That was the time period in which I had turned my life over to the Lord.

"Why?" I asked, dumbfounded at the "coincidence."

My mother explained that she had been praying as she walked down a city street in Toronto, Canada where she lives. All of a sudden, she felt a "presence" come up along side her. She immediately felt a strong sense of peace, as if the presence was trying to tell her that I was going to be okay.

Wow! How cool is that? God had reached out and touched a mother's heart 1,000 miles away, at the same time that her daughter was opening her heart to Jesus Christ. Is there anything our Lord can't do? He's awesome.

The spiritual interaction between the Holy Spirit and my mother and me, reminds me of John 4:49–53, wherein Jesus healed a government official's son. Despite the fact that the boy lay sick miles away in another city, he was healed in the exact hour that Jesus spoke the healing into existence.

> The nobleman saith unto Him, Sir, come down ere my child die. Jesus saith unto Him, Go thy way; thy son liveth. And the man believed the word that Jesus had spoken unto him, and he went his way. And as he was going down, his servants met him, and told him, saying, Thy son liveth. Then inquired he of them the hour when he began to amend. And they said unto him, Yesterday at her seventh hour the fever left him. So the father knew that it was at the same hour, in which Jesus said unto him, Thy son liveth: and himself believed, and his whole house. (KJV)

There were more revelations to come. The day after I was saved, I received a *literal* baptism. It happened while I was showering. The Holy Spirit filled me as I began to sing "Amazing Grace." An endless stream of tears combined with the water to cleanse me from head to toe, erasing my sinful past, and preparing me for my walk with Christ. Sheer warmth enveloped me. Again I felt that warm blanket of love, as though the Holy Spirit was wrapping his arms around me. Unconditional, Holy love was mine for the first time. I emerged from the shower, tears still flowing. Drunk with joy, I told Larry, "God just hugged me!"

For days on end, He kept revealing His presence and His power to me. I was so on fire for Him. Writing this now, I feel the rejuvenation of the Holy Spirit; remembering the intensity of the time I was born again. Don't you wish we could live in that state permanently? It was five years ago, but I can still recall how the Lord clarified my vision literally, spiritually, and mentally.

When I say literally, I mean that I can remember in between chemo treatments, bald as can be, with my little bandana and cap on, pushing Jake in the stroller, going for one of our mile-long walks. The whole time, I would praise the Lord for such a beautiful day; for the radiant colors all around us from the sky, to the flowers, to the trees. The colors were *literally* the clearest and most vibrant I had ever seen. I was a new creature in God, seeing with a clarity I had never experienced. The truth found in 2 Corinthians 5:17, was alive and well within me:

> Therefore, if any man be in Christ, he is a new creature: old things are passed away: behold all things are become new. (KJV)

But most importantly, on a mental and spiritual level, the Lord had blessed me with a new ability. In fact, I believe that every survivor, whatever the tragedy, is given a most precious gift: *the gift of clarity*. In an instant, our priorities, our purpose, our faith is clarified in a way that we may have never known, or appreciated, had we not had to walk through the fire. I just praise God for this blessing and for his ever-present love and support.

Not long after my first chemo treatment, I had the opportunity to testify at a tent revival. The Evangelist and his wife asked me if they could tape my testimony and use it to minister to the lost in the Kentucky Mountains. With that new clarity, that new sense of purpose, I told my story. And at the end of my testimony, I vowed to work for the Lord, from that day forward; to use all of my God-given talents for His glory.

Blessings During Treatment

The Lord continued to bless me during the next few months of chemo treatments. Other than the obvious hair loss, I still exuded a healthy, peaceful radiance. Not only was I able to care for my child, I was often able to take him for walks up to two miles a day!

I'll never forget the moment I sat in the hair stylist's chair to have my head shaved. As the razor made its way over my scalp, I testified to the stylist as to what the Lord had done in my life. When he finished, he said to me, "I've been in this business for many years and I've shaved the heads of many cancer patients. You are the first one who laughed and smiled the whole time you sat in this chair. Most of them cried." God is so good! My hair may have fallen to the floor, but He left me with strength, radiance and my sense of humor!

I must confess, however, that I did give in to vanity on one issue: I had accepted that I was going to lose my hair, but I asked God to spare my eyebrows. The thought of walking around, eyebrow-less, looking constantly surprised, was not very appealing to me. Can you believe he not only allowed me to keep my eyebrows, but he also left them *perfectly shaped?* You had better believe that I thanked Jesus for this blessing, and testified about it!

All kidding aside, whenever I walked into the chemotherapy clinic, I could always count on at least one staff member to tell me that I looked too good to be there. People at church commented on my radiance. And whenever I sent pictures to friends or family members, they would all say, "Besides the fact that you've lost your hair, no one would ever know that you have cancer. You don't look like a cancer patient." I would always reply: "It's the glory of God."

In the oncology community, there's a saying: "If the cancer doesn't kill you, the chemo will." A very important part of my exceptional health despite the toxic chemicals that were racing through my body, rested in the fact that again, the Lord had placed all of the right people in my life for a time such as this.

One of those people was Delana. She and I had become best friends 5 years before when we became next-door neighbors. Suffice to say that she and her husband, David, support during that time was absolutely integral to the treatment and recovery periods. While Delana was an emotional and spiritual rock, David's knowledge regarding nutrition and detoxification armed me with the tools I needed to stay as healthy as possible for my baby boy.

Don't get me wrong, my time with chemo was not a trip to Disney World. There were days when I felt puny and needed to rest. About two or three days after a shot of chemo, I felt like I was experiencing a hangover. But I was never once sick to my stomach! There is no doubt in my mind that following David's advice was integral to avoiding a lot of awful side effects, as well as my recovery. Delana and David are also Christians, so first and foremost, we all gave the glory to God for the miracle that was taking place. In addition, my oncologist was constantly dumbfounded by the speed at which my tumor was shrinking, as well as the absence of severe side effects of chemo.

Because of my faith in Christ, I never once asked my oncologist for a prognosis. As far as I was concerned, God was in control and no statistic could convince me otherwise. It wasn't until a few years later that I discovered the average person with my diagnosis had a 2% chance of survival...I'll take faith in the Truth over a statistic any day.

And thanks be to God for placing one of the finest oncologists and oncology staffs, especially the nurses who administered the chemotherapy that any cancer patient staff could have asked for. When I took my first cancer-related prescription to the pharmacist, she took me aside and assured me that she had seen a lot of good things coming out of that office. At that point, every little blessing counted.

Witnessing in the Midst of the Storm

Despite undergoing treatment, I was so thankful for what the Lord was doing. I shared my testimony with anyone who owned a pair of ears. I couldn't say enough about what Jesus had done for me and my family. And it was during this time that I was able to share the Gospel with members of my family in a way that I may not have been able to do otherwise. God was continuing to move in every aspect and every relationship that was involved in this journey.

As painful as it was to have to tell certain family members of my diagnosis, I was able to follow it up with the sweet story of my salvation. I was particularly close to my niece, Ally, who I love as a daughter. At the age of thirteen, she learned that her aunt had cancer, but she also learned that "I can do all things through Christ which strengtheneth me" (Philippians 4:13).

And after sharing my testimony with one of my very cynical cousins from Canada, he said, "I don't care if you have to believe in a rock to get through this thing..." Well, I did, and still do, believe in the rock that saved my physical and spiritual life, and His name is Jesus Christ!

It was as if a pebble had been dropped in the pool of God's grace and mercy and the ripple effect began. I was able to share my faith with believers and unbelievers, alike. And before I knew it, my family was included on prayer lists from Larry's hometown (New Orleans) to my hometown (Toronto, Canada).

We were covered up in prayer, and God's faithfulness was revealed once again. After the first round of chemo, the tumor had shrunk to *half its original size.* My oncologist was elated. "You're on the up curve," she said.

Claiming the Word:
God Shows His Mighty Power

It was three weeks after my second treatment, and I was walking the baby before getting ready to go to my oncologist. As I returned home, I met up with Julie and Kim (who was also a Christian). The conversation turned to the fact that we have authority over the enemy when it comes to our health. All along I had been praying along the lines of accepting God's will. I didn't realize that I had the authority to rebuke Satan and cast out any illness plaguing my body! As a child of God, as a believer in Christ, I had the power to claim my own healing. As told in Isaiah 54:5 (KJV):

He was wounded for our transgressions; He was bruised for our
iniquities: the chastisement of our peace was upon Him; and with
His stripes we are healed.

Christ had already taken on every affliction; every form of suffering in the world for our sake. For the first time I understood that the
devil had no power over my body!

I rushed home and before getting into the shower, I placed my
right hand over my left breast, rebuking the devil and any influence
he had over my body. Later that morning, Julie and I sat in my car in
the oncologist's parking lot, praying for a positive exam report from
the doctor. As we walked toward the office building, I turned to her
and said, "Wouldn't it be something if they couldn't find the tumor?
Let's believe for that."

Julie sat with me in the exam room. After examining me, the doctor smiled and said, "If this had been your first visit with me, I would
have told you that you don't have cancer. It just doesn't get any better
than this."

Julie and I beamed at each other. "Praise God!" we shouted.

We had received the news we had prayed for. Our prayerful words
had not returned void. Two faith-filled witnesses in an oncologists'
parking lot had appealed to our Lord, and He had answered; demonstrating His loyalty and His power. Another victory in this battle
had been won. Two were gathered in His name and He had been
right there in the midst of us (Matthew 18:20). Not only was the
cancer being defeated, the enemy was taking a beating as well! Isaiah
55: 11–13 comes to mind as I recall that joyous moment:

"…so is my word that goes out from my mouth: It will not return to
me empty, but will accomplish what I desire and achieve the purpose
for which I sent it. You will go out in joy and be led forth in peace;
…This will be the Lord's renown, for an everlasting sign, which will
not be destroyed." (NIV)

It was as though God was rewarding me for my obedience. I
had lived up to my part of the covenant, spreading the Good News

wherever I went; to anyone who would listen. I was exercising blind faith and reading His word daily, obeying the following truths:

(For we walk by faith, not by sight):

2 Corinthians 5:7, KJV

...so then faith cometh by hearing and hearing by the word of God.

Romans 10:17, KJV

During those three months of treatment, I prayed over my baby boy's crib nightly: "Lord, if you will see fit to let me live, I promise to raise Jake to be a good, strong Christian boy."

Meanwhile, my date with surgery was quickly approaching. I had been under the impression that I could have a skin-sparing mastectomy where the surgeons remove all of the tissue within the breast, but they leave the skin and insert the implant. Recuperation from that operation would be about a week.

At the last minute, however, I found out that I was going to have to have a radical mastectomy with reconstruction. That operation was much more complicated and required a three-week recovery. To say the least, this revelation left me a little unnerved.

Due to the length and nature of the recovery, my sister volunteered to come to stay with us and help take care of Jake. Not coincidentally, she too had been delivered from alcohol just before I was diagnosed, and believed that God was preparing her to take care of me during this time.

As for facing the more complex surgery, my only choice was to hold on to the belief that God had been with me this far, and He would carry me through the rest. I still had faith that the outcome of my surgery would be just as positive as my chemo treatment. But that would not be the case...

New Found Faith Tested

It was a beautiful fall morning when I checked into the hospital for a mastectomy with reconstructive surgery. In layman's terms, the procedure involves removal of the affected breast. A flap of tissue and muscle is then taken from the abdomen and is fashioned into the form of a breast. Using existing blood vessels for blood supply, the flap is then reconnected to the chest wall.

The upside of this procedure is that the patient receives an automatic tummy tuck in the process (yes!). The downside is that it is a fairly risky and complex operation. The pain and recovery time involved is more extensive than the skin sparing mastectomy. Unfortunately, it is the only option available to patients with inflammatory breast cancer because that type of carcinoma invades skin tissue as well.

To make a long story short, a projected five to eight day stay turned into a *seven week nightmare*. Due to the terms of a confidentiality agreement, I cannot reveal the details of exactly what happened. However, suffice to say that post-surgery complications left me with a spinal epidural hematoma (a 12-inch blood clot had formed on my spine), and I eventually lost the reconstructed breast.

I have described the excruciating pain I suffered at the time the clot took hold as electrical currents surging through my body *nonstop*. I would rather give birth to *ten* babies, *back to back, without an epidural* than experience that type of pain again. I was *literally out of my mind* with pain. I would like to add that this is not the experience of most women who undergo the mastectomy with reconstruction. It just happened to be mine.

When the paramedics arrived, they had to give me oxygen because I was hyperventilating due to the level of pain I was experiencing. For the first time in my life, I thought I might die. During the forty-five-minute ride back to the hospital, I begged the paramedic to give me something for the pain. He sat by helplessly and said, "I'm sorry. I can't. We have to wait until we get to the hospital." I couldn't believe it.

I'll never forget that when we finally got to the E.R., the admissions people were struggling with a software glitch. I was begging for help, and one of the men looked over the counter and said, "We've got a problem with the computer and you're just going to have to wait."

Hello! Here's a young woman, screaming in pain, her reconstructed breast had exploded and was hemorrhaging, and they tell me to take a number because they're having problems with their computer. It was like something out of a bad "B" movie.

However, once they found out I had cancer they admitted me, suspecting that the cancer may have metastasized to my spine. The nurse gave me enough morphine to knock a giant to his feet—it didn't even touch the pain. Despite the pain, some sense returned to me and I remembered that I had responded to another pain killer called delaudid. They pumped me full of that, and rushed me into the MRI (magnetic resonance imaging) tube. I was in there for over an hour as they scanned my entire body. I can remember thinking, "Wow, I'm really glad I'm so relaxed, because this would be hell otherwise." They finally found the blood clot and rushed me into surgery. It was 2 a.m.

When the surgery was completed, the neurosurgeon emerged from the operating room. A very good friend of mine at the time, Raina, had come to be with Larry in the waiting room. The surgeon explained my condition to them: the blood clot had been removed, I was going to live, but I was going to be a paraplegic. Larry was in shock. His wife, who had been his work-out partner for the last ten years, would never walk again. Raina later told me that she sobbed uncontrollably, bouncing off of the walls, walking through the corridors. The whole situation was surreal.

A Bedside Visitation

I spent at least a week in the Intensive Care Unit. I was so heavily sedated that I wasn't aware of the extent of my injury. My spinal cord had not been severed by the clot, but it had been squished enough to cause partial paraplegia from the waste down.

During those first few weeks in the hospital, Larry and my sister took turns between spending all day and night by my bedside, and then returning home to look after Jake. I will always be thankful for their strength and support.

When they finally moved me to my private room, the operating neurosurgeon came to see me...or so I thought. He told me that he was encouraged by the fact that the feeling in my right leg had returned so quickly and that I would eventually gain the use of my left leg. It would be a slow process, he said, but I would walk again.

The next day, however, the doctor returned with much different news. The bottom line was that I wasn't expected to walk again or regain the proper use of my bowels and bladder.

"That's impossible," I said, completely dumbfounded. "You told me the exact opposite yesterday."

"No, I didn't," he replied, equally confused.

I looked frantically at my sister, and Larry who were at my bedside. "You heard him yesterday. You were both here when he told me that my left leg would eventually come back and that I would walk again!"

To my amazement, and horror, they didn't confirm my recollection. "No, sweetheart," said Larry. "The doctor never said that. He just told us about all of this earlier this morning."

"No!" I insisted, addressing the doctor again. "You came in here yesterday and told me that I would walk again!"

"I didn't," he repeated, becoming uncomfortable and impatient.

"But, how is it possible that I remember an entire detailed conversation that never happened?" I asked, tears welling up in my eyes.

"I don't know," he said quietly, "but I never told you those things. This is the first time I have discussed your status with you. Now if you'll excuse me, I'll be back tomorrow to check on you."

As he left the room, the lump in my throat expanded until I burst into tears. This couldn't be happening! The Lord had brought me too far to have it turn out like this! There was nothing anyone could say to console me. I was numb. I cried and prayed off and on for the rest of the day.

I don't remember falling asleep, but I do remember waking up the next day rejuvenated and determined to believe the first diagnosis from the first "messenger." I don't know how long I laid there; praying and trying with every ounce of faith and strength I had to move one of my left toes. And then...it happened! Another miracle! One of my toes moved!

"Larry!" I shouted. "Look! It moved! It moved! My toe moved! It's moving! Do you see it?"

"Yeah! I see it!" he shouted, equally excited. He raced to the nurses' station and asked them to page the neurosurgeon.

The doctor came quickly. I wiggled my toe for him, and this time the tears were his. He was so excited he literally jumped for joy.

"You did a great job, doc," I said.

Tears welled up in his eyes as he pointed to the ceiling and said, "You have nobody but the good Lord to thank for this." It was now obvious that the neurosurgeon was also a believer. *Praise God!*

Today, I firmly believe, that the first messenger, the one who gave me hope, was either the Holy Spirit, or an angel sent by the Lord.

Off to Rehabilitation: Physical and Spiritual

The next step was a stint in the hospital's rehabilitation center. And yes, I was improving, but the emotional pain of being separated from my now seventeen-month-old son was almost unbearable. Jake was my motivation for waking up every morning and getting through each day.

But the shock of being in a wheelchair was so overwhelming that I virtually forgot about my battle with cancer. I had been so active and fit my whole life, even during cancer treatment. And then, boom! In an instant, my whole life had changed…I was a partial paraplegic. In a situation like this, you can't help but think, "This type of thing only happens to other people. It can't be happening to me."

How was I going to care for my toddler from a wheel chair? All I had asked from God was that I would be able to care for my son, and now even that had been taken away from me. In my despair, however, one of the scriptures that Julie had given me, Jeremiah 29:11–13, played over and over in my head:

> For I know the thoughts that I think toward you, saith the Lord, thoughts of peace, and not of evil, to give you an expected end. Then shall ye call upon me, and ye shall go and pray unto me, and I will hearken unto you. And ye shall seek me, and find me, when ye shall search for me with all your heart. (KJV)

The Lord felt so far away. I ached to find my way back into His

presence. Then one Sunday morning, after watching spiritual pro-
gramming for a few hours, I turned off the television and began to
pray, "Lord, let me bend my knee today. If I can bend my knee, I'll
have faith that I can walk again."

Again, I have no idea how long I prayed for. But glory to God,
after much effort and concentration I was able to bend my knee! I
was so excited! Larry and Jake would be there any minute for a visit
and I couldn't wait to show them.

That day, not only did I bend my knee, I was so pumped up, I
decided to try to stand. With a little help from Larry, I stood! We
were so elated, we both just stood there, hugging and crying. Jake
must have thought we were a couple of nuts. He looked at us as if to
say, "Big deal. I mean, yeah, you were excited when I stood up for the
first time, but this is a little bit over the top, guys."

The doctors and nurses had estimated a six-week stint in rehab.
But I was determined to be home within half that time. There was
no way I was going to spend Thanksgiving away from my family. I
continued to work hard and improved steadily with the Lord as my
strength and my little boy as my motivation.

During my hospital stay I was constantly inundated by visits, phone
calls, cards and gifts. But nothing could lessen the pain of being separated from Larry and Jake. I prayed constantly for relief from that pain,
but utilized it as motivation for getting stronger and getting out of there.
There were a few nights where I would call Larry at work and ask him
if he could stop by the hospital before he went home because I was in
desperate need of a hug. And God bless him, after working a ten-hour
day, he would show up and wrap those big strong arms around me, giving me the love and human touch I so desperately needed.

Constantly leaning on the scripture, Jeremiah 29:11–13, I finally
achieved my goal. After just three arduous weeks in rehab, a few
days before Thanksgiving, I finally returned home.

Home at Last

When Larry unloaded the wheel chair from the trunk of the SUV, I
told him, "Leave it in the basement. It is *not* coming upstairs." I had
just begun to use the walker and within a couple more weeks I had

graduated to a cane. I was, however, left with a lot of back pain and nerve damage which I continue to manage with medication.

One of the funniest and most touching moments of my homecoming occurred on Thanksgiving Day, just a few days after I was released from the hospital. As mentioned previously, one of my dearest friends at the time, Raina, and her boyfriend, were kind enough to prepare an incredible meal and bring it over to our home. Raina and I were lying on my bed talking just before dinner, when I gave a light-hearted directive: "Okay, no one is allowed to take pictures of the bald-headed chick with one breast and one leg." True to her gift of wit, without skipping a beat, Raina responded, "That's not true... you have one and a half legs!"

We laughed until we cried.

Blessings in the Midst of a Storm

While I was still in the hospital, Julie arranged for a number of my friends to get together and arrange for two-month's worth of dinners to be brought to our home. She also provided most of my daily transportation to and from the radiologist.

My step-daughter, Michelle, who was twenty-six at the time, was able to move in with us for several months to help me take care of Jake. *She* was also blessed during this time. Because she wouldn't have any bills while living with us, she would be able to go back to school to study massage therapy. The Lord also provided her the opportunity to personally witness my testimony. A seed had been planted there, and she continues to share my testimony with others.

Our blended family which also includes my twenty-one-year-old step-son, Chad, came together over this experience and emerged stronger. There are a lot of challenging issues confronting today's blended families; which is a subject matter for a whole other book in and of itself. But Jesus found a way to strip away all the unnecessary garbage until we found an appreciation and forgiveness for each other that had not been there before.

Life Today: The Blessings Continue

Glory to God, five years later, I am cancer-free and walk with only a slight limp. I still battle chronic back pain, however, and the pain and nerve damage is still controlled by medication. But had I asked for, and listened to, the World's prognosis for the cancer and paralysis, I most likely would not have survived, and at the very least, I'd be in a wheel chair.

Well-meaning friends and family insist that the Lord will heal me completely one day. I would love to be whole one day, to be physically restored and pain free. There are many moments that I wish I could teach Jake how to ride his bike, or play ball with him the way I had always dreamed of before he was born. I would love to run on the beach and jump through the waves again with my husband and my son. I would just enjoy not having to deal with all of the demeaning and discouraging side effects that most people would never even think were involved in dealing with a spinal cord injury. I'd be lying if I didn't admit that a complete healing would be an indescribable joy.

But, if that moment never comes, I can honestly say that the Lord's grace is sufficient for me. He's brought me this far, He'll carry me the rest of the way. And if it's His plan that I carry the thorn of my pain and disability as did Paul (2 Corinthians 12:7–10), then, like Paul, I will humbly rejoice in the fact that His strength will be made perfect in my weakness. If my testimony gives one other person the will to carry on despite their hardship, and brings them closer to Christ, it will be worth it.

In addition, I have been humbled and blessed by what the Lord has revealed to me in terms of the human spirit. Through it all, friends and family made themselves completely available to my family and me.

In 2003, we ended up finding and moving into a ranch home on a flat lot just north of Atlanta (the equivalent of finding a needle in a haystack). And, not surprisingly, God knew exactly what he was doing when he led us to this house. Just around the corner is an inconspicuous little Pentecostal church, pastored by the Godliest man I've ever known, Michael Abernathy. He and his wife, Shirley, have become mentors to Larry and I. We've been members of Creekside Fellowship Church for more than three years now and treasure our new church family. We continue our walk with the Lord, praising Him daily for His grace, mercy and many blessings He continues to pour out on our lives.

I have led a women's Bible study and have hosted our church's monthly television show on a local church channel. Entitled "Triumph over Tragedy," the hour-long show dealt with women's issues and how God's words and promises can overcome any tragedy...sound familiar?

Larry and Pastor Mike have formed a prison ministry that has seen over 2000 inmates saved over the course of the last two years, and have received an award for their efforts.

Together, Larry and I help out with the seniors and youth camp ministries.

Looking back, I've learned it's all about healing, about making that critical choice to turn from destruction...and then telling your story (testifying) so that others might be healed.

> He sent his word and healed them, and delivered them from their destructions. Oh that men would praise the Lord for his goodness and for his wonderful works to the children of men! And let them sacrifice the sacrifices of thanksgiving, and declare his works with rejoicing.
>
> Psalms 107:20–22, KJV

Today, I am living up to my part of the promise. The Lord has seen fit to heal me and my heart's desire is to declare His awesome works!

So, that was my intent when I approached Tate Publishing, LLC with the idea for *3T Vision*.

Because deep in my heart, deep in my soul, I have always known there was a book inside of me just waiting to be written. Even though I wasn't a "believer" at the time, I just innately knew it was a matter of time before *God* gave me the material.

God is so faithful and so good. The Holy Spirit was beckoning me the whole time, planting the seed. The lump in my throat grows and tears sting my eyes as I write. My heart is full, knowing that that "still, small voice" (I Kings 19:11, 12, KJV) was there even when I was a sinner. Thank you, Father, for your faith in me; for your love for me, long before I turned my life over to you.

So here it is: the *Vision;* the *3T Vision* that the Lord so graciously imparted to me, in order that I might share it with you. May you find comfort and healing as you read on through the next several stories, all testifying that *truth always triumphs over tragedy.*

> Blessed be God, even the Father of our Lord Jesus Christ, the Father of mercies, and the God of all comfort. Who comforteth us in all our tribulation that we may be able to comfort them which are in any trouble, by the comfort wherewith we ourselves are comforted of God.
>
> 2 Corinthians 1:3–4, KJV

Additional Scripture

*Theme: "God's protection in the midst of danger. God doesn't promise us a world free from danger, but he does promise His help whenever we face danger." (*KJV, LASB*)*

Psalms 91, 142

Jeremiah 16:9

*Theme: Praise for being saved from evil and certain death. (*KJV, LASB*)*

Psalms 18, 116

Theme: God's constant help—from childhood to old age. Our lives are a testimony for what God has done for us.

Psalms 71

Reflections

Chapter 2

Christy's Story
God Does Not Waste Miracles

From the Mouths of Babes...

...while Christy was speaking to her mother by phone about [her unborn baby's] inconclusive test results, she broke down and started to cry. When Leah came into the room, she quickly collected herself.

"Momma! Momma!" Leah shouted.

"Leah," Christy answered, "Mommy's talking on the phone."

In yet another prophetic instance, Leah interrupted again: "Momma! If God can bring that boy back from the dead, then He can heal [the baby] before 'she' gets out.

Later, Christy realized that Leah was recalling (Luke 7: 11–17) wherein Jesus raised a widow's son from the dead.

Christy: From that time on, I just tried to grasp that. I mean here was Leah, just five years old. If she could believe that God could do this, then I had to believe that myself.

Question: How many miracles can one person receive?
Answer: As many as they believe and ask for.

Ask and it will be given to you; seek and you will find; knock and the door will be opened to you. For everyone who asks receives; he who seeks finds; and to him who knocks, the door will be opened.

Matthew 7:7–8, NIV

The Interview

Despite the fact that I have known Christy for about two years (she is my pastor's daughter), I had no idea as to how many trials she and her husband, James, have faced during their seven years of marriage.

But that's Christy. You can't speak to the thirty-one-year-old mother of two for more than a few moments without recognizing that she's as wise as she is strong. Like a seasoned war veteran, you can see it in her eyes. You can hear it in her voice. But despite her "take charge," "git-r-done," attitude, there is an unmistakable humility about Christy's strength and confidence.

Her strength and wisdom is balanced with compassion, especially when discussing anything to do with children. Then, whether she's having an intimate conversation with one, or is standing before a congregation of 400, her voice will falter and tears will flow freely. She is one of her father's "right-hand women," second only to her mother, at Creekside Fellowship Church.

I'm sure that many people (including myself) have been guilty of assuming that if they had spiritual rocks for parents like Pastor Mike and Miss Shirley, they too would be firmly grounded in their faith. But Christy's faith doesn't come strictly from the love and support of her anointed parents; although that *is* part of it. Simply put: *she has earned it.*

In fact, Christy and James have earned their stripes in the "boot camp of faith" on more than one occasion. The analogy of "boot camp" is particularly applicable to Christy's story, and here's why: the purpose of any effective boot camp is to take an individual, break them down through a series of stressful exercises in a relatively short period of time, and then re-mold them into the "lean, mean, fighting machine" needed to win the war. In this case, of course, we're talking about a spiritual war and Christy has been on the front lines… many times.

In fact, when telling her story, it's hard to decide where to begin. Christy has fought battle after battle, and witnessed miracle after miracle. She describes the process as the "sanding down of a diamond"—that we can't be who God wants us to be until we have been molded by Him.

Often times that process can be arduous and painful. But Christy has exercised her 3T Vision and triumphed over tragedy more times in the past several years than most people do in a lifetime.

Through her journey she has learned to keep God first, her husband second and her children third. But her vision wasn't always that clear. It took seven years and many miracles to bring her perspective to where it is today. Her vision is simple: to be "all that she is called to be" in Christ Jesus.

We sat in my living room in the spring of 2006. As the tape rolled, I was constantly blown away by detail after detail of Christy's incredible, faith-filled story...

The Newlyweds Face Mortality

Christy and James had only been married a couple of months when she was given devastating news. Her pelvic exam and follow-up test had shown highly irregular cell growth. Before sending the sample out to the lab, Christy's gynecologist could not suppress her concern. The doctor was certain that her twenty-four-year-old patient had cervical cancer. She forewarned Christy that they would have to discuss treatment whenever the biopsy came back.

The first year of marriage is hard enough, as those of us who are married (or have been married) know. But these newlyweds immediately found themselves facing a life and death situation and the possibility that they may never be able to have children of their own.

In addition to their own prayers, Christy and James immediately summoned two of the mightiest prayer warriors in their family. They were going to leave no prayer stone unturned in this instance.

C: We just prayed about it. And my dad and my uncle came. They laid hands on me. My aunt called me and she prayed for me over the phone. She said, "Christy, we're just going to believe that when those tests come back, they're not going to know what happened. Those cells are going to be fine. They're not going to find any irregularities."

I said, "Okay." And we just agreed on it.

Three key components were alive and at work in this part of Christy's testimony: the *laying on of hands, belief* and *agreement*. When applied by the Christian heart, these three components have the ability to stop a freight train like cancer in its tracks.

First, they demonstrated their belief in the healing power of Christ's touch by laying hands on the afflicted body (Matthew 8:3, 14–15; Mark 1:40–45; Luke 5:12–16). Second, they *believed* that Jesus would intervene as in Matthew 8:13 wherein Jesus says, "Go! And it shall be done for you just as you believed it would" (KJV). Finally, they *agreed:*

> "Again, I tell you that if two of you on earth agree about any-thing you ask for, it will be done for you by My Father in heaven. For where two or three come together in My name, there I am with them."
>
> Matthew 18:19–20, KJV

Christy and her aunt had believed and agreed that God had the power to undo the preliminary report. In so doing, they confronted the devil's lies and applied truth to derail a potential tragedy.

Two weeks later, Christy and her mother returned to the gyne-cologist.

> **C:** [The doctor] said, "I don't know how, but those tests came back and they didn't even show inflammation!"
>
> I didn't have to take an antibiotic or anything!
>
> And Momma shouted, "We believe it's a miracle!"
>
> I was amazed! I just felt as though God had opened my eyes. And little did I know that was just the beginning. It was just one of the miracles that he would do in our lives.
>
> I know there are just so many people out there that are diag-nosed with cervical cancer. But I am such a believer that God can heal them. It wasn't something that was drawn out. It wasn't like the whole world was praying for me. It was just faith that He could do it, and the prayers of my family, and that was it. And [the cancer] is gone. There's no trace of it. It has never returned. It was truly a miracle.

Pulled from the Pit of Post-Partum Depression

As if to confirm His will, the Lord saw fit to bless James and Christy with a pregnancy just a few months later in January of 1999. Baby Leah was born in September. But the whirlwind in their lives was far from over.

As many women do, Christy began to experience a post-partum depression. But her case was so severe it threatened to destroy her marriage *and* take her life. At the time, however, she was not aware of what was wreaking havoc on her mind, body and soul.

As any new mother who works full-time can attest to, Christy was so busy, she didn't have a moment to sit down and analyze what was happening to her. Having been an over-achiever her entire life, Christy was beating herself up over the fact that she was over-whelmed by motherhood (all who can relate say "Aye"...And the crowd roared, "Aye!").

> **C:** I thought to myself, "Oh, my gosh! Why am I incapable of this? I have done everything else. I have succeeded in my life. Why can I not keep a house together and take care of this child?"
>
> Because there's this perfect wife/mother scenario that we feel we have to live up to. I felt so inadequate, as though I couldn't take care of what had been given to me. And I did not talk to James about it. I felt like I had let the world down. I was not allowed to feel this insecurity. And it was a perception that I had placed on myself. I had placed such high standards on myself. My job is what kept me together up until that point.

Finally, Christy bottomed out. Feelings of inadequacy turned to utter despair one night when the young mother actually contemplated suicide. Here was a woman who had felt God's love and had seen His miracles, yet at this point, she could not feel His presence.

> **C:** Then one night, Leah had been sick, and I was crying and crying and crying. And I remember thinking, "I could just kill myself right now." I was looking over at those razors, and I was thinking, "How can I get those out?" In my mind, I was battling, "I want to be a good mother to Leah, but maybe she'd be better off without me."

And I have all this training in mental health, so my intellectual side was saying, "Christy, you know you need to lay down. You need to rest. This is silly." But I could not quit crying.

If my life hadn't been so busy at that time, I would have fallen, and fallen *quick*.

As mentioned earlier, Christy was experiencing what is referred to as post-partum depression." (See end of chapter for complete definition). She describes the irrational and painful mindset she experienced:

C: I loved Leah. I loved her with all my heart. And it wasn't that I wanted to get rid of my life because I didn't love the people around me, or that I was in a bad situation, it was because I felt inadequate, like *I could not take care of what was given to me.*

In a desperate attempt to understand what was happening to her, Christy poured over her own mental health books and tried to follow their suggestions for dealing with depression. But because the hormonal imbalance was not being addressed, she finally "hit the bottom."

C: I hit the bottom of the bottom. Leah was about four months old and I had stayed home that day. And I remember packing up a duffel bag, full of her baby food and diapers. Then Leah had taken a nap, so it put me behind [schedule]. But I was going to put her in the car and we were taking off. I didn't care where we went. I was getting out of it. We were leaving because I did not need to be in that home, I was sick of being married. And I don't know why, because James is the most loving, understanding man in the world.

What may have happened to the desperate mother and her baby we will never have to know: because at that moment, in His perfect timing, God rescued them both.

C: God's hand was *so watching over me* at that moment. My hand was *right* on the doorknob when James came in. He asked me, "*What are you doing?*"

And I said, "I've just got to leave."

He asked, "Where are you going?"

"I don't know," I said. "I've just got to get out of here. I've got to try something new for a little while."

Christy had kept her emotions inside for so long, ashamed of her feelings of inadequacy and frustration. Now everything had come to a head. James was totally caught off guard.

C: James said, "Christy, you can go wherever you want to, but Leah is staying with me." And he grabbed her and he took her back in the bedroom. I just remember crying my eyes out because I couldn't let her go. There was no way I was going to leave without her.

That was all Christy remembers before waking up in the doctor's office the next morning. *She had passed out.* For those of us who underestimate the power of the female hormone, this story will rectify that. Her gynecologist determined that, because she had experienced continual post-partum bleeding since the birth of her baby, she was suffering from hormonal depletion. Although Christy had visited the doctor a few times over the course of the four months, they had assured her that the bleeding would eventually stop.

This time, however, the doctor prescribed birth control pills to stop the bleeding. The bleeding subsided and she felt as though she was getting back to her old self, but the emotional side of her struggle was still there. Then a whirlwind of personal crisis and activity followed.

Without revealing too many details (because I don't want to spoil the rest of the story) I can tell you that within the next two years: the couple sold their house and moved in with Christy's parents; James was seriously injured in an accident; the enemy would attack Christy again physically; and she was working full time while going to school, flying back and forth to Pennsylvania *every weekend* to work on her degree. Whew!

When everything finally settled down, and James had recovered, Christy had time to think. And before she knew it, that old dark feeling began to envelope her once again. Christy's feelings of inadequacy, mixed with extreme irritability and negativity challenged her marriage again.

> **C:** I [felt as though] I couldn't do anything right. And then it [shifted] to *James* couldn't do anything right.

At his wits end, once again, James begged Christy to seek counseling with him. At first her pride kept her from agreeing. Finally Christy realized that her irritability was out of the normal range. In addition, she was "working double time" to ensure that Leah wasn't aware of her feelings. Christy was bent on ensuring that her child's life would be "perfect and happy and that she wouldn't be exposed to any of the negativity." The young mother was emotionally and mentally exhausted.

On her own, Christy decided to contact a psychologist. She was finally diagnosed with post-partum depression. The doctor explained to her that serotonin, a neurotransmitter in the brain that influences mood, is carried in the blood. And because she had bled for so long after Leah's birth, her serotonin was totally depleted.

He further explained that people like Christy, who have an aggressive lifestyle, and go through multiple traumas in a short period of time don't crash during the activity because they're too busy to crash. It's when the activity settles down and they have time to think, that they tend to over analyze things, and they bottom out.

The doctor prescribed an antidepressant which would increase the level of serotonin in the brain and relieve the symptoms of her depression. Ever prideful, Christy didn't take the pills and kept the diagnosis a secret from James.

Battling feelings that she was educated and didn't need to take those "crazy pills," she knew that the negative feelings weren't hers. Deep down, she knew that she was struggling with an illness. Looking back, she credits the Lord for leading her to this particular psychologist. He knew that Christy would listen to this doctor, relent to her pride, and follow his advice.

> **C:** In this instance, [the Lord] used this doctor because He knew that I was "hard-headed," that I thought I was so educated, that I knew this

was going on. Because afterwards, I thought, how could I have been so stupid? I knew what was going on. But finally I knew that this wasn't me. I was dealing with a sickness and I had to try the pills.

Praise God, the effect was *immediate*. Christy's mood lifted. The difference was like night and day. All of the personal suffering ended when she finally discarded her pride and accepted help. Pride had been such a stronghold in her life. But knowing the scripture as she did, Christy was well aware of how God hates pride (Proverbs 8:13) and how pride goes before destruction (Proverbs 16:18). Her marriage was in peril. The Holy Ghost was convicting her and she finally gave in. The reward was immediate. God is good and He's *always* on time.

> **C:** I took one pill. I didn't tell anybody I had gone [to the psychologist]. I didn't tell anybody that I had taken the pill. The *next day*, James looked at me and he said, "Christy, something's changed." And I asked him what he meant. And he said, "It's just good to have you back. It seems like you've gotten your life back today." I just broke down and cried, apologizing and apologizing.

Ladies, we have to understand the power that our tongue possesses. While men develop their physical brawn to intimidate or manipulate their way through situations, women, the physically inferior of the sexes, have learned to develop their verbal skills. Speaking as one who struggles from time to time with this issue, we need to meditate on the following scriptures:

> For he that will love life and see good days, let him refrain his tongue from evil, and his lips that they speak no guile:
>
> 1 Peter 3:10

> Death and life are in the power of the tongue.
>
> Hebrews 13:8

(For more Scriptural references to the tongue, see "Additional Scripture" at the end of the chapter.)

There are numerous Scriptures in the Bible referring to the power of the tongue, which, to me, indicates the importance that God places on our responsibility to control it; to use it constructively instead of destructively. God wishes that our tongues produce honey, not venom.

Christy had finally taken responsibility for her tongue and the role that it was playing in the erosion of her marriage. Her irritability and constant criticism of her husband had passed the point of just being hurtful: they were ultimately contributing to the slow destruction of her marriage. Not only was she disobeying the above scriptures, but she was also in defiance of Ephesians 5:22 (NIV):

> Wives, submit to your husbands as to the Lord. For the husband is the head of the wife, as Christ is the head of the church. Now as the church submits to Christ, so also wives should submit to their husbands in everything.

Christy chose obedience and discarded her pride. After taking the pills for just one month, her serotonin levels evened out. She was able to discontinue the medication and has been fine ever since.

This deliverance was just another example of how, when we trust in Jesus and discard our pride, He will rescue us "out of a horrible pit, out of the miry clay, and [set our] feet upon a rock, and [establish our] goings" (Psalms 40:2, KJV). Our good and faithful God also gives us a new perspective or a "new song" (Psalm 40:3) when we wait on Him, as is evident in Christy's next discourse:

> **C:** It was a miracle that God sent me James because he is such a sta-bilizer, whereas I tend to fly by the seat of my pants. It was a miracle that he stayed with me through that year. I'm so thankful that he is a man of God and that he respected his marital vows. He was with me for better or worse. He didn't turn away. And when I would mention divorce, there was just no option of divorce to him. The only option in James' mind was that we work through it.
>
> God has had His hand on our lives for a long time. And every time I look back, I think about how He has protected me.

The Power of Prophecy

In hindsight, Christy recalls an evangelist visiting her father's church in 2001 just after James had had surgery. Not knowing Christy and James personally or anything that they had gone through, he prophesied that "what Satan had meant to destroy in [their] family, God would turn things around for the better and prosper [them]." This was yet another echo, another confirmation of the role that Romans 8:28 would play in their lives.

There were additional instances of prophesy that would plant seeds of faith for her and James to hang onto during the toughest of times: sometimes consciously, sometimes subconsciously.

> **C:** When I was going through the post-partum episode, there were a couple of people [at church] that came up to me and prophesied the spirit of depression. I would just not accept it. (Laughing) At times, I would say to James, "If they don't quit, I'm going to let them have it!" But, later on, when I got to that bottom point those prophesies gave me the edge to consider [seeking help].
>
> And about a year after James' accident (details to follow), he went up to the alter to receive the Holy Ghost and the gift of tongues. I went up with him. At that time, a member of the congregation prayed for me and said, "Christy, I know you're worried about this, but you're not finished having children yet. There will be another child." Leah was about three-years-old then.

For those of us who are unfamiliar with what the importance of the gift of prophesy let's look at what the Bible has to say: in 1 Corinthians 13:9 (NIV) Paul says, "For we know in part and we prophesy in part..." The study notes of said verse elaborate: "God gives us spiritual gifts for our lives on earth in order to build up, serve, and strengthen fellow Christians." Paul explains further, in 1 Corinthians 14:3 (NIV): "But everyone who prophesies speaks to men for their strengthening, encouragement and comfort."

Through the prophecies they received, Christy and James would find all three blessings!

The *truth* of how God was going to lead them to *triumph* throughout their lives, overcoming *tragedy after tragedy,* was prophesied in the *early* days of their trials! How good our God is to provide a message when we're in the valley of indecision! He may use a prophet, or something we're reading, or listening to, or watching on television, to confirm the *truth* that we know will get us through the darkest of times.

Often times we don't even understand the significance of the seed He is planting. It's not until we have a chance to look back and reflect that we truly see the wonder of His intervention. He is right beside us when we're battling the giants, and we may not even be aware of it. For as Romans 8:35–39 promises, nothing can separate us from the love of God in Christ Jesus.

In the end, we can look back and see that our ever faithful God *did* plant those seeds of *truth!* And those seeds of prophecy take root in our heart, giving us the courage, strength and peace we need to keep His *vision* of righteousness, His calling on our lives. And Praise God, we are more than conquerors! The enemy is defeated once again!

> **C:** Looking back I can see that God is so good and so true. Even though I didn't grasp that word of knowledge then, now I know it's true. Because honestly, there isn't anything we could go through together and not make it through now. God has blessed our lives and worked everything to our good (Romans 8:28). It was hard making it, but in the end, our life is better. Our hearts are healed, our marriage is healed. We have two healthy, beautiful children. There's just nothing else we could ask for.

God Prevails Over Pain

Note: For the faint of heart, the details surrounding James' accident are pretty graphic, so please be for-warned.

In the fall of 2000, James was working as a line crewman for Georgia Power.

When linemen ascend a hydro pole, they do so by nailing spikes into the wooden pole and stepping on them as they climb. On this day, the twenty-eight-year-old lost his footing on a loose spike.

Sliding approximately twenty feet down the pole, he landed on one of those pieces of plastic that you see wrapped around a cable located closer to the ground. The plastic cut clear through his protective straddle (brace yourself), effectively slicing his groin area in two.

Christy was in Pennsylvania when she got the call from her mother. The young wife, and mother of a two-year-old, had been flying back and forth to Pennsylvania State University while pursuing her Bachelor of Science in Occupational Therapy degree—no stress there! Christy flew home as quickly as she could.

> **C:** It was the beginning of two years of madness. [The surgeons] sewed everything back together and tried to save part of his testicles. But infection kept coming and going, and the sutures kept coming out. They wound up having to go back in and remove one of his testicles. When tested, it was determined that James had ten percent vitality. Anything less than twenty percent is considered sterile. The remaining testicle was intact, but it was bruised and traumatized, and there was a lot of scar tissue.

Anyone who knows anything about scar tissue knows that where there's scar tissue, there's *pain*. And where there's scar tissue in *testicles*, there's *unimaginable pain*.

> **C:** James was in pain for *two years*. He did not sleep for more than forty-five minutes a night. He could barely function at work.

In the meantime, the couple worked on rebuilding an older home they were going to move in to. As timing would have it, they sold the home they were living in and the buyers insisted on moving in within two weeks! So, Christy, James and two-year-old Leah, moved in to Christy's parents' basement until they could finish the house.

James would undergo two additional surgeries during this time, trying to repair the damage to his groin. Christy continued to fly back and forth to Penn. State every weekend. They couldn't have arranged for a more high-powered stressful time had they *tried* to orchestrate it. They had no alternative but to turn their situation over to Jesus.

> **C:** We prayed, and we prayed, and we prayed. Somehow, between God and my parents, we made it day to day. Now that I look back, I can't tell you the little things in life that we did [during that time period]. Those two years of my life were so traumatic. It's all just a blur in my mind.

Something had to give under such strenuous conditions. Christy's stress began to manifest itself physically in the form of chest pains.

> **C:** I was filling in for the director of a rehab unit for adults at the time. On this one day, my chest just started killing me. The pain ran down my arm, my face went numb, and I knew what that [meant].

Christy went to a co-worker and told her the symptoms she was experiencing. By this time, her teeth had started to go numb. Incredibly enough, she *waited to finish treating her last patient* before *driving herself* from Dalton to the hospital in Calhoun! Knowing Christy the way I do now, this did not come as a complete shock to me.

> **C:** I prayed the whole way. I could feel [my condition] getting worse. The numbness was traveling up to my eye and into my head. I said, "I rebuke this in the name of Jesus." And it stopped! (Choking back tears) It's so hard to describe how it felt, because I was thinking, "Okay, I'm either going to make it to the hospital, or daddy's going to come and find me on the side of the road," because I knew that he was trying to get there.

In her book, *Praying God's Word*, Beth Moore describes the power we have within us to claim our own healing:

> 2 Corinthians 4:13 says, "It is written: 'I believed; therefore I have spoken.' With that same spirit of faith we also believe and therefore speak." If you are in Christ, you have been given that "same spirit of faith." The original word for spirit is literally translated "breathe." When you speak God's Word out loud with confidence

in Him—rather than your own ability to believe—you are breathing faith. Believing and speaking the truth of God's Word is like receiving blessed CPR from the Holy Spirit. (38)[2]

What a perfect description of what it means to believe and to speak the truth of God's Word! At her very core, at that defining moment, Christy had claimed God's truth in Jesus' name and triumphed once again. She had literally received CPR from the Holy Spirit, stopping a "stroke in progress" in its tracks. It was done for her as she had believed (Matthew 8:13).

Ironically, James had just had an operation and wasn't able to meet his wife at the hospital. By the time Christy arrived at the emergency room, the left side of her face was drooping. Her arm was numb and paralyzed. The twenty-five-year-old told the doctor that she suspected she was having a stroke.

But glory to God, the electrocardiogram showed only mild irregularities and her blood pressure was only slightly elevated. After stabilizing her, they informed Christy that she had most likely had a mild stroke.

You would think this experience would slow her down a bit. Not Christy. "Droopy face and all," she returned to work *three days later!*

C: I *had to!* I had to keep going. It took about a month for my face to get back to normal, and I eventually got the strength back in my arm. But I had to change some things in my life. Here I was, doing homework until one in the morning, getting up at 6 a.m., dropping my child off at daycare, going to work, flying to Penn State on the weekends, renovating a home, selling another home...and all while James was sick! I was living day to day, not realizing how much stress I was under. But I think that God was also showing me that He could heal me because He had healed me before.

I think we can all relate to that struggle we have with our flesh when we're in the midst of struggling with any sort of illness. But we have to pray our way out of that sort of mindset and *believe* Hebrews 13:8 which says: "Jesus is *the same* yesterday, and today, and forever" (KJV).

There would be yet another healing in store for the couple. This time, *James* would ask and receive. James had been dealing with the pain of residual nerve damage for two years. Christy had come to accept that this was just something they were going to have to manage, still hoping that the doctors would eventually figure out how to remove the scar tissue that caused so much discomfort. But several procedures later, James continued to suffer. Unbeknownst to Christy, James was quietly working on his own faith for his healing.

> **C:** He's not a person to beg for anything. He's not going to do that. He doesn't complain and constantly let you know [that he's hurting]. But you could see it, and you knew it.
>
> Then one day there was an evangelist who came to our church. For two years, James never went up for prayer for [his injury]. I think that he believed that if God was going to heal him, He would do it on His own, and not through someone else.
>
> James was at the end of his rope. He got up and went to the front of the church to get prayed for. I couldn't believe it.
>
> He told the evangelist that he was in a lot of pain and needed a healing.
>
> The evangelist prayed over James and told him that in three days his pain would be completely gone. When he came back to his seat, he told Christy, "It's done." (*Praise God!*)

As they walked out of the church, James claimed his healing, telling Christy that he was feeling a lit bit better.

> **C:** He took that word, and he accepted it. He was so positive. I wanted to believe it, but I just couldn't see it. It had been two years.

And praise God, again! *That night,* for the first time in *2 years,* James slept for *eight hours.* Christy woke her husband up the next morning with the excitement and anticipation of a child on Christmas morning.

C: I asked him, "How do you feel?! Do you feel any different?!" And he said, "Yeah, yeah! I feel pretty good! I feel great!"

I mean, I could tell by the way he walked that he was still in some pain. I watched him like a hawk all day. And usually at night he would take a pain pill before he went to bed, but that night, he did *not* take a pill.

The next morning, I asked him if he was feeling any better, and he said he was. Finally, after the third night without taking a pain pill, he got up and cut the grass! And I said, "James, are you feeling better?" He told me, "Christy, [the pain] is gone. Every bit of it is gone."

And that was it! It was over with!

Later that week, James and Christy met with the urologist who happened to also be a believer. They told him what had happened and that James was no longer in pain. The doctor confirmed the fact that it was miracle, because there had been nothing else the medical community could have done for him.

The couple readdressed the issue of whether or not they would be able to have any more children.

C: He told us that James' tests had come back at 10% which was considered to be infertile. But then he said, "You just never know, though. You've had one miracle; maybe you'll have another one."

The Cherry on the Cake: The Miracle Baby

C: We had gone on a trip to Maine in the summer of 2004. We had tried to explain to Leah that we weren't going to be able to have another child because James had been hurt. We told her that we might adopt, but that we weren't able to have any more of our own.

But true to her resolute roots, Leah was not going to take "no" for an answer. She wanted a baby sister and she was going to have a baby sister.

C: I guess it was toward the end of the school year when Leah told her Pre-K teacher that she was having a baby sister. (Laughing) And

I got on to her, saying, "You can't go around telling people Momma's pregnant when she's not."

During that time, Christy was working as an occupational therapist in the public school system where she lives in Northwest Georgia. One of the children had tested positive for the Cytomegla Virus.

If passed on to an unborn child, CMV has the potential to affect the unborn child's brain. Among a litany of affects, the child can be born mentally retarded, blind, deaf, etc. At that moment, Christy had no reason to be concerned: James was sterile; they weren't going to have any more babies, end of story. But God had another plan. And it all started with four-year-old Leah's declaration from the back seat of their Lincoln Town Car.

> **C:** We were riding in the car traveling from New York up to Maine, and I was sick as a dog. I thought it was because I had eaten a hot dog out of one of those vending machines. I laid my head down on Leah's lap in the back seat of the car, and she said, "Mommy, I think you have a baby in your belly."

Christy reassured Leah that there was no way that she had a baby in her belly, that she was probably just sick from the hot dog. But anyone who knows Leah knows that if Leah's sure about something, she's not going to quit until everyone else knows it too.

So when they reached their destination in Maine, Christy and James decided to buy a pregnancy test, despite the fact that the closest Wal-Mart was an hour and half away! They made the drive, bought the test, and there it was…that ninety-nine percent accurate, undeniable pink strip! Normally this would have been a moment of all-out rejoicing…but the moment was tainted by the realization that Christy had been exposed to CMV.

> **C:** It was a miracle! But then I thought, "Okay, it's a miracle that I'm pregnant but I was really upset because I knew that I had been around this other child who had CMV. And I guess, because I was in the field [of occupational therapy]; I was overwhelmed because I knew the implications of that.

When they returned from their trip, Christy immediately went to see her obstetrician.

C: There are different levels that show up on the test, and it showed that I had been infected with the virus. But the *level* that showed up was in between "yes" and "no" in terms of the baby being negatively affected.

At this point there was a lot of uncertainty regarding the implications for Christy's baby. Not only were the levels uncertain, an ultrasound needed to be done to determine how far along she was. If Christy had contracted the virus after the first trimester, her body would have had time to generate enough antibodies to protect the fetus from contracting the virus. Under those conditions, there would be a good chance that the baby would be born healthy.

C: When they did the ultra-sound, it appeared that I was *three and a half* months pregnant. The baby *looked okay,* but the [viral] test had come back positive. And I guess that I stress that [the levels] were "in the middle" because nobody could tell me if the child was going to be okay.

The situation had "border-line" written all over it. It was an excruciatingly emotional time for James and Christy. They were torn between having been given a miracle child, their concerns regarding the virus, and keeping the mood elevated around Leah who was so excited about having a baby "sister."

C: I was just beside myself and so was James. He was terrified. I think it was worse for him because, even though I knew what could be in the future, he had no idea because he had never worked with a child who had had [the virus]. It was so hard because here is this child, and you don't know if it's going to be born with so many disabilities. You question whether or not you should go through with the pregnancy.

Knowing God the way they did, however, Christy and James could not believe this was a cruel joke played on them by nature. It had to be another test of faith.

> **C:** (With tears welling up.) Satan just comes against you, trying to influence your decisions, trying to make you see, that even though I'm a therapist, and I love special-needs kids, and I would never harm one of them. But then there was the thought that, "Now it's going to be *my child* that I'm going to have to go through this with." So we stood in faith. I believe with all my heart that it was God's plan that I didn't know that I was pregnant [when I found out about the virus] because by the time I found out the results [of the CMV test], abortion was not an option.

It's as though the enemy knows your most tender spot and sticks a hot coal in it, trying to cast doubt and fear into your belief system. He goes after your heart of hearts, and Christy's heart is with children and their special needs. If he was going to get to her, if he was going to strike fear and doubt into the depth of her soul, this was the way to do it.

On the lighter side of things, if that was at all possible, the ultrasound had also indicated that the baby was a boy. Once again, however, Leah was insistent that the doctors and their technology were wrong. No matter how many times the doctor tried to explain the difference between the "hamburger" and "turtle shell" images, Leah would not budge. She was having a baby sister and that was the end of it.

Because Christy was already into her second trimester by the time the pregnancy was discovered, the next several months seemed to fly by. Test after test was performed. In the process, Christy and James consulted three specialists, all of whom confirmed that she had tested positive for the virus.

> **C:** But again, they couldn't tell us with any certainty how the child would be affected: the reason being, that the baby would be most affected during the "acute infection period" of the virus and it was hard for them to pinpoint when that stage occurred in terms of the actual date of conception. At that time, there was still some infection

showing, but the test results at that point could not determine the severity of the affects of the virus, if any at all.

Christy and James dug their heels in and stayed grounded in their well of faith. Again, abortion was not an option. It was a daily battle with the enemy for their hearts and minds. It was clear that man could not provide them with the answers they were looking for. Could they continue to believe for the unseen, for the supernatural instead of the natural? In their reservoir of hope, Christy and James hung on to what they *knew* God was capable of. And if the baby were to be born disabled, His grace would be sufficient (2 Corinthians 12:9).

> **C:** I had to find courage. One part of me was trying to accept that my child might have this [virus]. I had to find comfort in my own expertise that I could deal with it, that I knew what to do for the child. It wouldn't be so bad because I knew what to expect. But then the other half of me was just trying to hang on to that little bit of hope, that it would be born [healthy].

Here again, the flesh and the spirit were at odds. Satan is a liar, but he includes just enough truth to make his lies believable *in the flesh*. Christy could have given in to the temptation to give up hope, resigning herself to the fact that she was equipped to care for a disabled child. Again, it was a daily battle to fight the good fight of faith.

> **C:** We had to get on with life; we had to have faith. If Leah had enough faith, we had to believe that everything would be okay. We had to put up a barrier against the mental, emotional and spiritual stronghold because it was such a burden. It was just best not to acknowledge the magnitude of the situation anymore for Leah's sake.
>
> We knew we weren't going to get any answers from the medical community. We couldn't torture ourselves with "what if" anymore. We had to believe. It was all we had left. If the doctors couldn't give us any answers, we *had* to believe for a miracle.

While they tried to shelter Leah from the precarious nature of the pregnancy, Christy and James did have to address the issue of multiple doctor visits.

> **C:** We told her that the baby might be sick and we didn't know exactly what to expect when the baby was born. But we also told her that we had to believe that the baby would be fine. And she seemed to be okay with that.

Then one day while Christy was speaking to her mother by phone about [her unborn baby's] inconclusive test results, she broke down and started to cry. When Leah came into the room, she quickly collected herself.

"Momma! Momma!" Leah shouted.

"Leah," Christy answered, "Mommy's talking on the phone."

In yet another prophetic instance, Leah interrupted again: "Momma! If God can bring that boy back from the dead, then He can heal 'her' before 'she' gets out.

Later, Christy realized that Leah was recalling Luke 7:11–17, wherein Jesus raised a widow's son from the dead.

> **C:** From that time on, I just tried to grasp that. I mean here was Leah, just five years old. If she could believe that God could do this, then I must believe it myself.

Early in the pregnancy, Christy and James had decided to keep the precarious nature of her pregnancy under wraps from most people. Although Christy went up for several alter calls and it was clear to our congregation that "something" was wrong with the pregnancy, we respected her privacy and just simply prayed for the family.

> **C:** If it was true, I just wanted to hide under a shell and not come out.

A very private and dignified person, Christy did, however, consult with her closest family members, including her grandparents. Bot-

3T Vision: Truth Triumphs Over Tragedy

tom line, the baby's condition, the decisions regarding the pregnancy, would be determined once again, by their faith, by their relationship with God. But, as evident in other *3T Vision* stories, I truly believe that God sometimes uses people to deliver messages to us.

Christy's paternal grandfather, affectionately known to all as "Pop" would not accept it.

> **C:** He told me there was nothing to worry about, that it was going to be okay. Things would work out.

It's worth saying here that "Pop" is a dead ringer for Santa Claus. He has that unique mixture of quiet warmth and strength that is so reassuring during a crisis. He doesn't speak much, even when consulted, but when he does, it's impossible not to take what he says to heart.

Christy also sat down with her grandmother and step-grandfather, a.k.a.: "Nanny and Pa-Pa."

> **C:** "Pa-Pa" is a very intellectual person. He looks at everything, puts it together and then analyzes it. In his quiet way he sat back and he told me that, "God doesn't waste miracles." And I believed that deep in my heart, that if God gives you something, there's a reason. God doesn't make mistakes. I had to believe that God was going to protect [the baby].

Despite her faith, Christy was a human being facing the daunting possibility of having a disabled child. And despite the many miracles she had seen within her own family and the church congregation, there were times when she and James just had to resolve to make it through the day.

> **C:** Even though I believed in my heart that the baby was going to be okay, sometimes, when you're at the bottom, it's hard to see that God can perform one more miracle. That's when you have to go back in and find that quiet place with God, taking time to remember all the miracles He has worked. It just takes you back to [remembering]

all the miracles that he has worked. It makes you wonder why you would doubt that he could perform another one.

So fight that doubt we must, because doubt is the devil's play-ground when we are in spiritual warfare. We know how the enemy lurks about, seeking to steal, kill and destroy. But we also know that Christ came to give us life and life more abundantly (John 10:10). Christy continued to fight the good fight, clinging to the measure of faith that God had placed in her (Romans 12:3, NIV). She had to believe that "God did not waste miracles."

The moment of truth had arrived. God's miracles were far from over, even during labor and delivery. Christy's best friend, Annette, stood by during the entire process. Not only was she a blessing in terms of emotional support, Annette also happened to be a nurse. Her presence in terms of Christy and the baby's physical condition proved to be another example of divine intervention.

> **C:** Annette was such a blessing. I had tried to send her home. I was so exhausted, so tired from the anesthesia. The nurses were young and new. But Annette would come in, wake me up and say, "Christy, you need to turn over, your baby's heart rate is going down."

Finally, Christy went into full labor. When the baby began to emerge, the doctor lost the heart rate. When it was finally delivered, the umbilical cord was wrapped around the neck and body. Had Annette not been there to rotate her, Christy is sure the baby would not have survived. God is so good! But wait, there's more!

> **C:** When the baby came out, I asked, "Is he okay? Is he okay?" And the doctor said, "No, he's not okay." I just fell apart. I started crying. And I was so upset because Momma and Daddy and everyone were smiling and laughing. I thought, "This child's been born and we've had all of these problems. Why is everyone laughing?"

And James came over to me and he said, "Christy, what's wrong?" And I said, "[The doctor] said he's not okay." And James said, "No! He said, '*He's* not okay, but *she* is! It's a *girl!* She's fine! She's healthy!"

Today, they can look back on that moment and laugh. Because of the cheerful din, Christy had been unable to hear the latter part of the doctor's declaration that the baby was not a boy after all, but a healthy baby girl.

So not only was the baby born healthy, four-year-old Leah's prophecy had been realized! Even on the drive over to drop Leah off at Pop's house on the way to the hospital, Leah had insisted that she was about to have a baby sister.

Truth Triumphs: A Family Grows In the Spirit

> **C:** I thank God for Leah. She is a miracle in and of herself. She was such a support. And Julia's healthy and happy and a perfect little girl. Now I thank God for the way things did happen. I can't imagine what life would be like if we had aborted [the pregnancy] and not had her here.

I mean, it was just a miracle from the beginning to the end. And all I could think of was, "how could I have doubted that God could do this for us?" Sometimes you think you're so small, or so inadequate, but it doesn't matter. God can work a miracle for one person just as much as he can for someone else.

Christy is admitting in her ever humble way, a mindset that many Christians wrestle with. No matter how often God proves Himself in our lives, sometimes, even if just for a fleeting moment, we lose sight of the supernatural and fall back on our natural world asking, "Can He *really* come through for me *again?*" Think about the disciples who finally knelt before Jesus after he walked on water, rescued Peter from the waves, and then silenced the storm (Matthew 14:29–33).

There have got to be times when Jesus must shake his head at us and say, "Hello! Let's get with the program, people and make a decision! You're either in the boat or you're out of the boat! How many times do I have to prove myself and bolster your spiritual insecurities?"

Only when we realize Jesus' true character will we truly believe that He will be there with us through every storm. But we have to have that truth deep within us before we can triumph over life's tragedies with a quiet confidence, knowing that Jesus is by our side. We don't have to cower in the corner of the boat. We don't have to sink beneath the waves.

In the *Battlefield of the Mind Devotional,* Joyce Meyer includes a chapter on this very subject. The prayer she includes at a chapter's conclusion is worth repeating here:

> Lord Jesus, sometimes I'm like one of the fearful disciples, requiring all kinds of proof before I can believe You. How many miracles do I need to see before I can call You the Son of God? Help me to be more like Peter, ready and willing to walk with You in any and all storms of life. Thank You for loving me and encouraging me to follow You in faith. Amen. (185)[3]

Christy has learned what we all must come to terms with: circumstances can shift. Life is full of positives and negatives. The enemy will do his best to throw in as many negatives as he possibly can. Consequently, every family has their ups and downs. We live *in* the world, but we don't have to be *of* the world. It's a daily battle.

We have the Power to get off the roller coaster. As Christians, we must remain constant in our *faith* and our *vision.* With God's *truth,* we can boldly stare Satan in the face and *triumph* over any *tragedy* he throws at us. Christy describes how her daily approach to life has changed as a result of her refined faith:

> **C:** Even if I wake up and I'm not in the best of moods, I'll try to make it a point to say something nice, or uplift one of them in some way, or do something special for [my family]. Because I feel like God has given me a second chance [at motherhood]. The devil tried to steal [our joy] with the first one. And I am bound and determined that my second chance is not going to be wasted. [Satan] is not going to defeat us.
>
> Sometimes you just have to make yourself look at the positives. There are times when James and I will be on the verge of getting

upset about something, but we'll just look at each other and start laughing because now we know that's *going to be okay.*

Key to this new outlook was restructuring her priorities. Prior to her first pregnancy, Christy admits that her priorities were: career, mother, wife (a pit many of us fall into when we've worked hard for our degrees). Now she realizes that God's *vision* for our priorities as Christian women, and the one she is now committed to following, is: God, husband, children.

C: God showed me that James is my help-mate. He is the one who helped pull me through all of this. He's my partner—the other half of me. I have to take care of *him* in order to provide my children with the environment they need at home. James and I need to be the example to them of what they want to be. Now, we try to find *our time,* even if it means just finding an hour together after the kids have gone to sleep.

All through these tragedies, God has shown me what's real, what's *true,* what the core of my foundation should be. It's about trying to find that quality time. And now I'm okay with not making $100,000 a year. I'm okay with exchanging less money for more time.

Going through these tragedies and emerging triumphant changes who you are. It refines you. It shaves away the roughness and finds the core, the essence of who you are. You'll find your strength. You'll find yourself. You'll learn to trust in God and those around you instead of being totally independent and self-absorbed.

It still surprises me that so many people come to me and James for advice, despite the fact that we're so young. But I think they recognize what we've been through. It's as if we have about 15 years of experience packed into those 2 tumultuous years.

God has used what was meant to destroy us, not just to prosper us, but to enable us to reach out to others.

Sometimes we're required, as was Christy, to go through that refining fire. Sometimes the pain of that fire is the only thing that will force us to discard our pride and reach out for the *truth.* Only then can we step back, let go, and let God work in our lives. Only then can we fulfill the calling, the *vision* that He has for us.

> **C:** We learned a lot. I think it makes you stronger. And hopefully we'll get to the point where we won't question God and we'll just accept that His plan is the perfect plan for our lives. And even though we don't believe that it's going the "right way," it's what He has planned for us, and we'll be stronger people for it. We're called to live from faith to faith.
>
> I think each miracle and the way that you live it, the way you experience it brings about such a change. Your belief becomes so much deeper, so much of an emotional part of you, because you ask, "How could this happen to us? Why did he choose us [for these miracles]?"

But He did choose the McDonalds. And I have a feeling that God isn't close to being through with this family yet. To know them is to know that the Lord has a special calling, an incredible anointing on this family.

Triumph Brings Peace
And Blessings for Others

Today, Christy and a leader from another local church head up a children's summer camp ministry. "Camp JAM (Jesus and Me) is a non-profit organization to provide the youth of North Georgia a place to enrich their relationship with Christ.

The activities are designed to empower the kids to become the people that God has called them to be: mentally, physically and spiritually. Adult volunteers act as spiritual mentors and camp counselors.

Christy continues to work as a contracted occupational therapist while juggling her responsibilities as wife and mother of two. James is in his sixth year with Georgia Power and has just completed his Associates degree in Business and Accounting. He is also a Sunday school teacher and deacon at Creekside Fellowship Church.

C: Our life is so peaceful now; it's so different. The trials we faced, our experiences, have made us strong in our faith, with each other and with Christ. We've been through so much, that when we go through something now, we have the realization that God is going to take care of it. We *know* that God is in control.

Now, even though we're busy, we don't have the mental stress of worrying. Whatever happens in the future, we'll know that it's God's plan for us; that we will be exactly where we're supposed to be. It's a peaceful, comfortable place to be.

Additional Scripture

Theme: to believe for the spiritual instead of the carnal world
Proverbs 3:5–6
Zechariah 4:6b
1 Corinthians 2:14
Hebrews 11:3

Theme: Crying out to God in times of despair (holy fear); recognizing that we can't do it on our own.
Isaiah 59:19b
2 Chronicles 20:3–4, 7, 12
Psalm 42:5

Theme: Focusing on God instead of on our problems; He will reward those who diligently seek Him.
Psalms 119:48
Proverbs 4:20–22, 23:7
Ephesians 4:23

Special Note:

WebMD.com describes "post-partum depression" as:

"...a serious medical condition that can develop some time in the first few months after childbirth. Without treatment, PPD can be prolonged and disabling. PPD is very common, affecting 1 in 8 women during the first months after childbirth. PPD can also strike after miscarriage, still-birth and adoption.

In rare cases, a woman with postpartum depression also develops psychotic symptoms that endanger her and others (postpartum psychosis.)

Symptoms of postpartum depression include extreme fatigue, loss of pleasure in daily life, sleeplessness (insomnia), sadness, tearfulness, anxiety, hopelessness, feelings of worthlessness and guilt, irritability, appetite change, and poor concentration.

PPD seems to be triggered by the changes in hormone levels that occur after pregnancy. These hormonal changes are especially likely to lead to postpartum depression if you've had depression before, have poor support from your partner, friends, or family, or are under significant additional stress.

Every woman has a risk of postpartum depression during the first several months after childbirth, miscarriage, or stillbirth. Women with a history of depression or postpartum depression have an even greater risk. A personal or family history of bipolar disorder, also known as manic-depression, increases the risk of postpartum psychosis...

PPD is best treated with counseling, certain antidepressant medication or a combination of the two...Some women gain significant relief after a week or tow of starting treatment with either medication or cognitive behavioral counseling."

(For more information see www.webmd.com/hw/depression)

Reflections

Chapter 3

Melissa's Story
"Be Still and Know That I Am God."
(Psalm 46:10, NIV*)*

...do not worry about tomorrow, for tomorrow will worry about itself. Each day has enough trouble of its own.

Matthew 6:34, NIV

...the emotionally fragile woman inserted her key into her car door when an inexplicable feeling washed over her. Minutes later, a delivery truck would slam into her Plymouth Horizon, rolling her car three times. Witness accounts say they heard the rescue team call in a D.O.A. victim. But, GLORY TO GOD, the paramedics were able to revive her and rush her to a local hospital. Melissa's life and those around her would be forever altered.

Before my accident, I was very independent and very strong-willed. I did everything for myself and it was always 'my way or no way.' And I had a big mouth about everything.

Well, God [was going to use my car accident]. There I was, lying in my hospital bed. I couldn't even go to the bathroom by myself. I had to wear

*diapers until I could finally get up and walk. I could not feed myself. I had
to have someone feed me every meal.*

*God knew the humble place to which he had to bring me, before I would
realize that I couldn't do anything on my own. I had to come to the realization that "I'm not God. I can't fix it."*

Melissa

The Interview

Melissa and I became acquainted, as many mothers do, through
our children. Jake and Rebecca attended the same Christian School
through Pre-K and Kindergarten. They became fast friends immediately, pushing each other on the swing-set all recess long. Well, let
me clarify that: Rebecca loved to push Jake on the swing and he was
more than happy to oblige...

Even though we would get together and talk during school func-
tions, it wasn't until Melissa invited us to Rebecca's fifth birthday
party that we discovered how much we had in common. It's sad that
in today's world, we are so busy, our schedules so jam-packed, that
if we're not careful, we can miss out on receiving blessings that the
Lord has planned for us.

But, Praise God, I was able to slow down and attend "Becca's"
birthday party with Jake. Married for eighteen years, Melissa and
Richard (a contract assessor and preacher) are the proud adoptive
parents of two beautiful Korean children: Andrew, age six and Becca,
age five. Nestled at the end of a quiet cul-de-sac in the Atlanta sub-
urbs, their home is complete with a gigantic playground area and
newly purchased camper parked out back.

Several other adoptive parents were on hand with their South-
east-Asian-born children as well. They are all members of Colorful
Families, a support group comprised of parents who have adopted
children from overseas.

Once the kids were busy burning off the birthday cake and ice
cream playing on the enormous "jungle gym," Melissa and I had an
opportunity to talk. We shared our testimonies and the fact that I
had just signed my first publishing contract. Realizing immediately

that her story could contribute to the concept of *3T Vision,* we made plans to get together for an interview.

The following story is yet another example of how God will demonstrate his faithfulness in the midst of a catastrophe, and that he can turn all circumstances around for our good and His glory (Romans 8:28). And as Melissa explains, His only requirement of us is that we "Be still and know that [He is] God." (Psalm 46:10, NIV)

In its entirety, Psalms 46 reads so powerfully. Written by the Korah (temple assistants), this psalm describes our God who is an all-powerful and our ever-present fortress; "He will never fail to rescue those who love him" (1144, NIV)

> God is our refuge and strength, an ever-present help in trouble.
>
> Therefore we will not fear, though the earth give way and the mountains fall into the heart of the sea, though its waters roar and foam and the mountains quake with their surging. *Selah*
>
> There is a river whose streams make glad the city of God, the holy place where the Most High dwells. God is within her, she will not fall; God will help her at break of day. Nations are in uproar, kingdoms fall; he lifts his voice, the earth melts.
>
> The Lord Almighty is with us; the God of Jacob is our fortress. *Selah*
>
> Come and see the works of the Lord, the desolations he has brought on the earth. He makes wars cease to the ends of the earth; he breaks the bow and shatters the spear, he burns the shields with fire. "*Be still, and know that I am God;* I will be exalted among the nations, I will be exalted in the earth."
>
> The Lord Almighty is with us; the God of Jacob is our fortress. *Selah*
>
> Psalms 46:1–11, NIV

Is there anything our God cannot do?

Tough Choices: God Rewards Obedience

In the spring of 1986, Melissa was working part-time during her sophomore year at Kennesaw State College, in Kennesaw, Georgia. This should have been an exciting time in the life of a nineteen-year-old. She should have been full of hope and aspirations. But Melissa was at the end of her emotional rope.

After finding out about her daughter's involvement in a local Baptist church, Melissa's fervently Catholic mother had issued an ultimatum: either leave the church or leave the family. Melissa returned home one night from a meeting with the church's Singles Group and was unable to open the door to her family's home.

> **M:** I had recently joined the Baptist church and I was going to be baptized there. I went back to my mom's house. She just pulled the curtain back from the door window and asked, "Did you join that Baptist church? I don't want a 'damned' Baptist living in my home." When I told her I had joined the church, she told me I was no longer welcome in her home. I tried to open the door, but realized she had locked it with the deadbolt. I did not know what to do. I was devastated.

Not knowing where to go, Melissa drove to her best friend's house. Tisha's parents also happened to be Melissa's Sunday school teachers. After recounting her mother's absolute rejection of her, they offered Melissa a place to stay. When church staff members and "empty-nesters," Bob and Sheila, learned of Melissa's predicament, they offered her one of their vacant bedrooms.

Isn't that just like our God? When we step out in faith, and stand up for Jesus, he will stand up for us. Because, contrary to Catholic doctrine, she chose to stand firm on Jesus' commandment that we must be born again in order to see the kingdom of God (John 3:3, NIV).

At that crucial moment, Melissa could have taken the path of least resistance, sparing herself the discomfort and uncertainty of having to support herself completely at this time. But she knew in her heart that God always makes a way for the obedient. She chose to trust God and believe in His truth. And our ever faithful Father blessed her, providing a supportive Christian home for Melissa to live in while she finished school.

Little did Melissa know, this period would prove to be the "calm before the storm."

Humility: The Tough (But Valuable) Lesson

Even more emotional strain was just around the corner. Melissa and her then boyfriend, Richard, decided mutually to end their six-year courtship. Both were adamant about their religious beliefs and neither was willing to budge. While he had been raised in a "foot-washing" fundamentalist Baptist church, the doctrine at Melissa's church represented a more progressive approach to Baptist worship.

In addition, Melissa was deeply saddened by the fact that Tisha had recently become engaged, and had moved away.

So in a short period of time, she had lost emotional support on three separate fronts. On a beautiful spring day, the emotionally fragile woman inserted her key into her car door when an inexplicable feeling washed over her.

> **M:** I was supposed to be a bridesmaid at Tisha's wedding. I was just so depressed. I remember putting the key into the car door and saying to myself, "Tisha, I'm so sorry. But I'm probably not going to make it to your wedding."

Minutes later, a delivery truck would slam into her Plymouth Horizon, rolling her car *three* times. Witness accounts say they heard the rescue team call in a D.O.A. victim. But, glory to God, the paramedics were able to revive her and rush her to a local hospital. Melissa's life and those around her would be forever altered.

> **M:** I had a severe head injury. I was in a coma for *nine days*. When I woke up I had immediate short-term and long-term memory only. I had no recollection of the several years leading up to the accident. And all I knew was that I wanted Richard. I had no memory of our break-up or the fact that I had been dating someone else briefly before the accident.
>
> And I'll never, ever forget sitting in the rehabilitation center, trying to feed myself for the first time. I [was covered in] food from

my head to my knees and I was crying, "Please momma, please help me!" But the doctors had told my mom not to help me, because I needed to learn how to feed myself. So for a while, I just cried. I had to wear a [body-length] bib.

Matthew 18:4 illustrates this part of Melissa's journey:

Whosoever shall humble himself as this little child, the same is greatest in the kingdom of heaven.

Our Lord, the ever-loving Potter, literally reduced the once self-sufficient, all-knowing, young woman into a totally dependent child. But once reduced to that ultra humble state, Melissa had a choice to make: she could stubbornly continue on in that self-sufficient, know-it-all mode, or she could learn to rely on Him. She made the choice to rely on His truth to carry her through the tragedy and on to triumph. The once "tougher than nails" clay, was now pliable in His hands.

M: He just taught me that I need to be submissive to Him and rely on Him for all things. I needed to see that I didn't need to be head strong, and gung-ho for myself, because I can't do anything anyway without Him.

Rehabilitation: Hanging On to the Vision

When she was finally released from the hospital, it was decided that Melissa would convalesce at her mother's home in Alabama. Even though it made the most sense for her to be there for logistic reasons, her spirit yearned for the nurturing of her church family.

She would spend three months in Alabama, undergoing extensive rehabilitation. There were so many reasons, so many opportunities to give up and give in to the spiritual and physical demands being placed on her. She found herself in a spiritually barren wilderness, isolated from the love of her Christian brothers and sisters.

M: I was so discouraged. Here I was in Alabama, with my Catholic family who didn't like me being Baptist in the first place. I was away from all of my Singles friends. I didn't have my church family to encourage me. They told me that I couldn't go out [on my own], so I didn't have a driver's license. I had a new psychiatrist, a new physical therapist, a new occupational therapist, and I was going to a strange hospital where I didn't know anybody.

And my family drank. I could have just sat there and drank all my problems away. But I never did. I kept holding on tightly every day to the fact that God was going to get me through. All I had was my Bible and I had the phone. I studied my Bible every single day. And the one scripture that I repeated every day was, "Be still and know that I am God" (Psalm 46:10).

In addition, Melissa relied on the many pieces of scripture that her Christian counselor, Vinny, had given her before she had left for Alabama. The Lord had placed this beacon of light in her life for such a time as this. A very wise and Godly man, Vinny had counseled Melissa through many trials, and he would prove to be instrumental in her recovery as well.

M: He brought me through a lot of things. He would just always say very positive things. He told me that the Lord would always be there for me, that the accident happened for a reason, and that [the Lord] had a purpose for my life.

Realizing that Melissa was about to leave her support system, Vinny had taken it upon himself to create a "life preserver" of sorts to compliment her Bible study. On a pad of paper, he had written Scripture for each day with room for her to record her thoughts and feelings.

Oh, how the Lord works! What a precious opportunity Melissa had been given! To "be still" and able to commune with God, to study His word and "draw nigh to him" for three months! How many of us struggle every day to find just 15 minutes alone with the Lord for Bible study, prayer, or worship? She could have spent three months brooding and feeling sorry for herself in that bedroom in Alabama. But instead she pursued and meditated on His truth.

She had a vision for a productive life that she was not willing to give up on. And she knew that Jesus would be there for her, to carry her over to a better place. Like Naomi, forced by tragic circumstances to return to her homeland, Melissa resolved to stay true to her Lord and place her life in His capable hands. And true to His nature, the rewards would be forthcoming.

In fact, while Melissa was busy studying, praying and writing, the Lord was busy softening her mother's heart. The once overbearing and inflexible woman was beginning to recognize the miracle that her daughter's Lord had performed. He had returned her once vegetative-state daughter to a functioning human being in a relatively short period of time. And she was improving daily!

> **M:** I think that after my mom had seen the miracle that God had performed on me, in bringing me back to an actual human being who could do things for herself, she began to let up on me a little bit. She saw that I had trusted in the Lord, and put all my faith in Him. And so she quit demanding that I return to Catholicism.

Melissa's mother finally accepted her daughter's conversion to the Baptist faith, allowing her daughter's faith to "take root and thrive." This change in heart meant less stringent rules being placed on Melissa as she continued to heal. Her mother agreed to allow her to spend the occasional weekend at Bob and Sheila's, attend church, and reconnect with her Singles friends. Her friends were also able to visit her at her mother's home as well.

Melissa credits this reconnection with her church family as one of the main things that inspired her to persevere through the emotionally, mentally and physically grueling months of rehab.

Again, being faithful to Him, trusting in His truth, and waiting on his word allowed God the time to work all things out for her good and His glory (Romans 8:28).

Not only was Melissa's mother convinced of her faith, her brothers and sisters began to follow suit. In fact, four of her five siblings carried the process a step further and actually converted to the Protestant faith!

> **M:** Once I was married and living a healthy lifestyle, they could see

that God had miraculously healed me and blessed me. I really feel that that had a big impact on them.

Melissa had obeyed Christ's commandment to boldly proclaim our faith in Him; unashamed and unafraid. Pride had prevented those around her from coming into a direct relationship with Christ. And because of this, Melissa had met with condemnation and criticism. But she obeyed God and made the decision to turn away from man's methods and turn toward His great weapons of prayer, faith, hope, love, truth, and the Holy Spirit (Ephesians 6 :13–18). By doing so, Melissa was able to fight the spiritual battles before her:

(For the weapons of our warfare are not carnal, but mighty through God to the pulling down of strong holds);

Casting down imaginations, and every high thing that exalteth itself against the knowledge of God, and bringing into captivity every thought to the obedience of Christ; And having in a readiness to revenge all disobedience, when your obedience is fulfilled.

2 Corinthians 10:4–6, KJV

In the midst of her turmoil, she was bearing fruit for the kingdom: a direct result of what happens when we focus on Christ instead of our problems!

Instead of wasting away in loneliness and isolation, instead of abandoning the faith that she had so strongly adhered to before her accident, Melissa made the choice to grab hold of the tools the Lord had provided. Instead, she chose to "put on the whole armor of God" (Ephesians 6:11) and *bolster,* not abandon, her *3T Vision.*

The Armor is Tested (Go Figure!)

Then in 1986, tragedy struck again. Betrayal reeled its ugly head when it was discovered that Melissa's best friend, Karen, was having an affair with the church Pastor. Still struggling to recover from her accident, Melissa was utterly devastated. And to add insult to injury, some members of the congregation assumed that because of their close relationship, Melissa must have had knowledge of the affair. It was "guilt by association."

> **M:** [Karen] never confided in me. She never told me anything about [the affair].
>
> I was emotionally scarred by that. I was very close to both of them. I loved them both. How they could have torn the church apart like that was beyond me.

Still emotionally and physically fragile, Melissa found herself embroiled in the scandal. She struggled to make sense of it all: the Lord had provided a miraculous healing, relationships were being rebuilt, and she felt closer to God than ever before in her life. Yet the enemy seemed to be lurking, attempting to undermine her testimony (John 10:10, KJV).

> **M:** I knew that Satan didn't want me to give all the glory to God. He tried everything he could to make problems for me, so that I would ask, 'Where is God in all of this?' I felt as if I had been dealt a double-whammy. I was so affected by the scandal.

During this time of emotional and spiritual distress, the Lord provided solace once again in her mentor and counselor, Vinny. And physically, the woman who had once lain comatose, with little or no recovery in sight, continued to grow stronger every day.

Faithfulness Rewarded: Relationships Mended

So while her church experienced a period of disintegration, the Lord blessed Melissa with a season of integration. Rewarding her resolute faith, He was bringing her mind, body and soul back into a healthy alignment. Oh, praise the Lord, for he is good! He continued to pour out His blessings on her life, and her countenance radiated God's favor.

So much so, that even Richard and his family members began to sit up and take notice. The once all-important conflict over religious ideology began to melt away. All that mattered was that the Lord had seen fit to perform a miracle. And as it often happens, that one miracle had a domino effect, rolling from a physical healing to the healing of her once fractured relationship with Richard.

> **M:** [Our] religions were so totally different. I think [the miracle] had such a big impact on Richard's family and how they saw it; that even though I wasn't going to the church they thought I should go to, the Lord was still blessing me.
>
> I think the whole experience helped Richard see that even though someone might worship in a different manner than he did, it didn't make them any less of a Christian.
>
> It is so unreal that I am not brain damaged today. And I still thank God every single day for waking up sane and being able to understand everything. Because at one time, my mind was that of a child, and [Richard's family] could see how far He had brought me.

Melissa admits that the religious conflict continued years into the marriage, but it did not carry the weight that it originally had. Their renewed appreciation and devotion for one another was strong enough to hold the relationship together, but more had to be done.

Her walk with the Lord was maturing to the point where she realized the next step to solidifying their marriage would depend on her ability to become submissive to her husband—a feat that would challenge her very ingrained, independent sensibilities (sound familiar ladies?).

But Melissa's devotion to the Lord finally superceded her fleshly desire to remain steadfast in her religious ideologies. And once she was able to break that strong-hold, she says the blessings in her marriage began to flow.

> **M:** Even when Richard and I were dating, we had arguments all the time. I was not going to let him take the lead. I was not going to listen to him about anything. I was going to do everything for myself.
>
> Then the Lord brought me to a point where I couldn't do anything for myself, so that it would become easier for me to be submissive. And even now, I find it easier to be submissive. Every time I start thinking, 'No, I'm going to do it my way," I say, "Wait a minute. [Richard] is the head of my household. And I need to be submissive

to him." God says that he is the head of the wife and God is the head of [the husband]. And that's the way it's going to be from now on. And it's easier for me to see it that way now.

When I finally humbled myself enough to do what God wanted me to do, I decided to [adopt Richard's manner of] worship and be submissive and raise my kids in that way. And we've been a lot happier ever since.

In hindsight it's clear that, from the beginning of their relationship, the enemy was trying to divide and distract them from the future missions God had planned for them. But their faith, and Melissa's resolve to turn to the Truth for answers, thwarted the enemy's every advance. As difficult as it was for both Richard and Melissa to compromise their positions, they knew that if their relationship was going to survive, they would have to be obedient to God's Word as written by Paul in Ephesians 5: 21–26, 33:

Submitting yourselves one another in the fear of God.

Wives, submit yourselves unto your own husbands, as unto the Lord.

For the husband is the head of the wife: even as Christ is the head of the church: and he is the savior of the body.

Therefore as the church is subject unto Christ, so let the wives be to their own husbands in every thing.

Husbands, love your wives, even as Christ also loved the church, and gave himself for it...

Nevertheless let every one of you in particular so love his wife even as himself, and the wife see that she reverence her husband.

A Dream Fulfilled

Although their relationship continued to thrive and mature over the next eleven years, the couple's efforts to have a child were fruitless. When the obstetrician suggested a laparoscopic procedure to determine the cause, Melissa put on the brakes and turned to the Lord for guidance.

> **M:** I was just convicted in my heart to pray because after my car accident, I really felt convicted that the Lord wanted me to go into missions overseas. I was always touched by Asian children because that would [involve] reaching the world. Whenever I saw an Asian child, I wanted to reach out to them, to share Jesus with them.

After marrying Richard, however, Melissa's dream of becoming a missionary had been put on the back burner. For more than a decade she struggled to understand why the Lord would put two convictions on her heart that seemed to be in conflict with one another.

But God's thoughts are not our thoughts and his ways are not our ways (Isaiah 55:8–9). When Melissa learned to trust God and obey His truth concerning her marriage, He blessed her with the fulfilling of her vision.

So after years of trying unsuccessfully to get pregnant, and with desire in her heart still burning to reach out to Asian children, Melissa took a leap of faith. In their eleventh year of marriage, she asked her husband to pray about adopting an Asian child.

> **M:** Adopting was the furthest thing from Richard's mind. And, I'm telling you, it took nothing but the Lord to convict him of it.

But again, the couple trusted in the Lord to provide, to make a way. And He did. Over the next few years, Richard and Melissa would bring home two children from South Korea: Andrew and Rebecca.

The couple discovered an adoption agency that specialized in the adoption of Korean children. The agency's approach was unique in that the adoptive parents were not required to fly overseas and spend an extended period of time fulfilling the adoption process.

Instead, Richard and Melissa would meet with a local social worker who would screen them and acquaint them with the child through photos and information from the child's file. If the adoption went through, the child would be flown to Detroit where the expectant parents would pick them up and bring them home.

M: I was so convicted in my heart to adopt an Asian child. So I
prayed that if it was God's will, that He would open the door and let
it all go smoothly…And it did. It all went like clock-work.

Not long after, the couple met with the social worker. The file told
the story of a young, un-wed Korean woman who was unable to care
for her son. There were two pictures of the baby boy enclosed. Richard and Melissa took the pictures home with them. They wanted to
pray over the pictures and consult the Lord as to whether or not this
was the child who was intended for their family.

M: The next morning, Richard said he had a "light-bulb go off in
his head" while he was in the shower. He just knew that Andrew was
the one to adopt.

The excited parents-to-be immediately contacted the social
worker to follow through with the adoption plan. After everything
was approved, it was off to Detroit to pick up their baby boy: eight-
month-old Andrew.

While most people make a mad dash to the hospital on the day of
delivery, Melissa and Richard drove to the Atlanta Hartsfield Airport to catch a flight to Detroit. (Think about it, ladies! Her delivery,
her excitement, would not be dulled by the agony of labor pains!
Now *that's* what I call a "double portion" blessing!)

M: The day we flew to Detroit to pick up Andrew was the most
exciting day of our lives. We found ourselves in a strange airport,
holding a sign that bore our last name.

And then we saw this little Asian lady carrying a baby. Andrew
had his little head resting contentedly on her shoulder. And when
she handed him to me, the first thing he did was lay his head just
as comfortably on my shoulder. It was just as if he'd been sent from
heaven…and he was!

Andrew slept through the entire flight back to Atlanta. It was ¾
of the way through the flight before I would part with him and let
Richard hold him. The whole family was waiting for us at Hartsfield
when the plane landed. It was just so incredible.

Perhaps because of his age, Andrew's adjustment went as smoothly overall as it did at the airport. In contrast, two-year-old Becca was more cognizant of the abrupt changes taking place in her world and her relationships at the time of her adoption. The resulting emotional turmoil, coupled with what would have been a challenging time of adjustment anyway, began to take its toll on the family.

It was as if Melissa had instantly given birth to twin "terrible two-threes!" Between sibling rivalry and adjustments to the family dynamic, a near disaster was averted when Melissa turned to prayer and the Lord's promise: "if ye shall ask anything in my name, I will do it" (John 14:14, KJV).

> **M:** I called everyone I knew, and asked them to pray for us. And it worked! I'm telling you! You just don't know how much the Lord has worked in these children! They were little angels sent from God. They're wonderful. And I give God all the glory for it.

The once frazzled mother prayed for peace and sanity to prevail in her home. Today, her prayers continue, but, praise God; they've taken on a different tone.

> **M:** I get down on my knees every day and pray for [Andrew and Becca]. I drop them off at school, and when I get home, I pray, "God, let them have a good day. Don't let anybody hurt their spirit. And please surround them with your spirit each day."
>
> I'm not saying that lightly, either. I take praying for my children very seriously every day. I believe God has blessed me for that. He has kept his arms around them and he has held them. And I'll continue to pray for them every single day that I live.

In retrospect, Melissa believes her calling to missionary work has been fulfilled with the intricate intercession of the Holy Spirit. What she did not understand before, the two seemingly contradicting convictions that He had placed on her heart, makes perfect sense to her today. Like Naomi, like Mary and Elizabeth, Melissa remained obedient to the Lord in the midst of turmoil. She had faith in the truth and kept her eye on the Lord. In the end, she was rewarded with the realization of her vision and triumph over her tragedy.

> **M:** In a way, I feel like I'm doing something with missions! I'm reaching Asian children, who I wouldn't have reached had I not married Richard and adopted. I wouldn't have been able to share Jesus with these children. And trust me; my kids know that whenever they're afraid they can call on Jesus. I've impressed on my children that He can be everything to them...everything!

Still Standing on the Rock

Oh how the good Lord works! In order for Melissa to be the mother and wife that she is today, in order for to fulfill her vision for missions, the Lord saw fit to capitalize on a tragedy and reshape her from a child-like state to a woman whose heart it has been to serve Him, first and foremost. Once she put Him first in her life (something many of us need to work on), the blessings came forth and the vision was realized.

Melissa believes the car accident was God's way of saying, "I'm going to put you in a place where you will have no choice but to "be still." Unfortunately, for some of us (your humbled author included), the Lord knows it will take something very dramatic to get our attention. And, depending on the strongholds involved, some pruning can be more painful than others. She describes how the effects of the accident brought her to her spiritual knees, bringing her to that a humble state in which the Potter can begin to reshape the mound of clay.

> **M:** Before my accident, I was very independent, very strong-willed. I did everything for myself and it was always 'my way or no way.' And I had a big mouth about everything.
>
> Well, God used that car accident, and there I was, lying in my hospital bed. I couldn't even go to the bathroom by myself. I had to wear diapers until I could finally get up and walk. I could not feed myself. I had to have someone feed me every meal. God knew the

humble place to which he had to bring me, before I would realize that I couldn't do anything on my own.

And I never would go to him with the little things before. I'd say, 'Oh, never mind, it's not like it's a tragedy or anything.' But then I realized, 'No! God wants me to come to him with everything in my life.' And I know that because 1 Peter 5:7 says "cast all anxieties upon Him because he cares for you." So that means everything!

My life had been a testimony for the Lord, all the way through. I just can't impress upon people enough how much the Lord will provide for you if you will just depend on Him.

How much truth there is in this last statement! For instance, how many times have we recited the Lord's Prayer? Probably enough that we almost become unconscious of the meaning in the passage, "give us this day our daily bread" (Matthew 6:11). When we recite this prayer and that particular passage, we are acknowledging that we depend on and trust our Father *for our every sustenance.* We deceive ourselves if we believe that we are our own provider. Only God has the power to fulfill our daily needs, *according to his plan and purpose.*

M: I can't even really begin to tell you of the blessings he has given me. I used to feel so unworthy of Him. But I'm beginning to realize that we have to believe we are the person Jesus thinks we are. We can't have low self esteem because Jesus doesn't [want] that for us. We can't think we're any lower, or we'll miss the blessings He has for us.

Melissa continues to rely on the key pieces of scripture, the rock that she set her foot upon to bring her through her darkest of hours.

M: I still repeat Psalm 46:10 every day, "Be still and know that I am God." And if [we] could just sit still sometimes and say, 'Lord, you are God and I am not. But I can do anything, because 'anything is possible through Christ Jesus' (Philippians 4:13, paraphrased). So I'm just going to [sit] here still, and know that you are going to bring me through to the other side–to a better place than I am right now.' And He *does*. He *always* does–whether it's the big things or the little things.

As often happens, the immediate tragedy and catastrophic results may have seemed insurmountable had Melissa not had the faith to overcome. But she kept the *vision;* she kept her eye on the light, during the darkest of hours. And the Good Lord, the Master Weaver, would connect each intricate piece of her life's tapestry into a fully functional and beautiful quilt.

Today Melissa is a wife, mother, friend to many, and volunteer at her children's school. But first and foremost she is an "on-fire" woman of faith whose exuberance for the Lord is contagious. Her "cup overflows" in every conversation I have ever had with her. She is passionate about every aspect of her life, personifying the promise, the truth, that we have been given "life and life more abundantly" (John 10:10). Melissa's triumph is a shining example of what can happen when we *choose life;* when we *choose truth,* in obedience to Him.

Additional Scripture

*Theme: Our ultimate strength is in the Lord (*KJV, LASB*)*
Isaiah 40:31
But those who wait on the Lord shall renew their strength. They shall mount up with wings like eagles, they shall run and not be weary, they shall walk and not faint.

*Theme: Humility (*NIV, LASB*)*
Importance of humbling yourself before God: (Joshua 7:6)
Stops quarrels (Proverbs 13:10)
Gives you a more accurate perspective of yourself (Obadiah 4)
Recognizing God's work in you (1 Corinthians 15:9–10)

Reflections

Chapter 4

Karen's Story
From Blind Trust To Clear Vision

I was totally alone in the backyard, absolutely miserable, and as soon as I said, "I don't understand it, I don't like it, I'm afraid of you, but I'm going to accept Jesus as my Savior," I had an ecstatic joy. And that was a new feeling, because I had never in my life felt happy. I didn't know what that feeling was. I knew it felt wonderful. I didn't even know words to describe it. We didn't have happy words in our vocabulary. We lived with such sorrow and blame and shame and guilt.

That was definitely the greatest experience of my life as far as having a "happy feeling." The only other time I ever felt that way was when my father died because then he would not be a threat to my daughter who was just four months old at the time. I was so relieved that I wouldn't have to worry about him being around her.

Karen Austin: abuse survivor

> None of you shall approach to any that is near of kin to him, to uncover their nakedness; I am the Lord.
>
> Leviticus 18:6, KJV

The Interview

When Karen and I met at her office one morning to conduct the interview for this book, it wasn't the first time I had visited her there.

The past year of my life had been particularly stressful, and for the first time I relented and sought counseling. Discussing the matter with my family doctor, I was adamant about two requirements for my potential counselor: they would have to be a female and be a Christian.

After following up on my doctor's recommendation, I found myself at the offices of Crossroads Counseling, a private Christian counseling service owned by Karen Austin, a Licensed Christian Counselor and Therapist.

She is such an insightful and effective counselor, it's hard to believe that she has only been in practice for four years. Maybe that's because she has also spent the past fifty-five years in the school of hard knocks and faith building. Her story as revealed in her book, *Blind Trust: a child's legacy,* is powerful, disturbing and inspirational.

For anyone recovering from, or studying the effects of childhood sexual and emotional abuse, I strongly recommend you read the book. *Blind Trust* is a personal memoir, giving a close-up look into an abused child's world—a world filled with pain, confusion and the pervasive effects of child abuse.

Be forewarned, it's a very intense read in some areas. For those of you who are still raw with emotions and memories concerning the abuse, I would recommend first and foremost that you receive counseling if you haven't already.

It's no surprise that Karen's area of expertise lies in counseling both adults and children who are recovering from trauma and are experiencing Post-Traumatic Stress Disorder (a type of anxiety disorder that can develop after a person experiences a traumatic event).

In fact, on the day that we sat down to conduct the interview, Karen was preparing to take a ten-hour flight in order to testify in a parental sexual-abuse case. Even though she was struggling with some pretty serious health issues that involved substantial pain, Karen was determined to follow through on her commitment to testify. The attorney involved had indicated that her testimony would be vital to the case.

"I've flown in pain before. I can fly in pain again," she said, laughing heartily. "What are a few days out of my life if I can make a difference in the life of a small child?" She paused for a moment, and continued: "You know, we had Animal Rights Protection laws in the 1800's, but we did not have a law to protect children until the 1970's. And even now, it doesn't really protect the children. It's more about parental rights;" hence, her choice of careers.

She's a woman with a mission. She's a woman with a *vision*. Despite the fact that she was horribly abused from the time she was a toddler, Karen's deep desire was always to be a mother—to nurture others, to love and be loved. Perhaps that was because the first thirty years of her life were devoid of all those things.

But God is a big God, His love is unconditional, and again, all things are possible through Christ who strengthens us (Philippians 4:13, paraphrased, KJV). Every day Karen triumphs over her personal tragedy. Her faith-based counseling is part of the fulfillment of her vision to help those in need of understanding and protection. She is also a published author, working on her second inspirational, self-help book.

The following story follows one woman who turned to God's truth and emerged from a devastatingly abusive background to become a faith-filled Christian counselor.

"I Was Important!"

One hundred years from now it will not matter what kind of car I drove, what kind of house I lived in, how much I had in my bank account, or what my clothes looked like. But the world may be a little better because I was important in the life of a child.

Author unknown

Dysfunction with a Capital "D"

(As in Karen's book, *Blind Trust,* most of the names have been changed to preserve confidentiality.)

Lester and Rose Smith and their four children appeared to be the epitome of the small-town, church-going family during the 1950's and early 1960's. When she wasn't busy beating her children with her husband's belt, Rose loved to proudly parade her children in front of the community in the town square during special festivities and parades. The family could never convince their father to attend special events with them. Rose would tell the children that he was "too busy drinking himself into oblivion," to accompany the family. The mother and her four children were much more relaxed in his absence anyway.

Civil Rights marches were the talk of the day, while Children's Rights were at least a decade away from being realized. This would be a misfortune for a little girl named Karen Smith who suffered unmentionable abuse behind the doors of her family's poverty-stricken and morally bankrupt home.

> **K:** I basically grew up in a family with every type of dysfunction you can imagine: poverty, religiosity, sexual abuse, physical abuse, and of course, emotional abuse. Everything was very secretive. We weren't allowed to have any activity outside of the family, because my father was afraid I would "tell." He was an alcoholic. My mother was mentally ill.
>
> I was the next to the oldest of four kids, and I was the only girl. Micah was the oldest, then me, then Randy and then Jeff. My parents treated the boys differently. My mother was a firm believer that women were put on this earth to serve men, and that we would do all of the work that needed to be done.
>
> I had my first surgery at the age of three and then many surgeries after that to correct the damage from sexual abuse.

Sadly enough, despite the fact that many people must have suspected what was happening, nobody chose to stand up for the shy, sickly, "scared-of-her-own-shadow" little girl.

> **K:** The societal view at that time was, "You don't mess with family matters." So, nobody really did anything. In fact, it was always the "blame the victim" mentality. My mother was actually angry with me for costing them money to have the operation. She did not have the courage to see my father for who he was. But now as an adult looking back, I realize that she was mentally ill. I don't know that there

was anything she could have done differently. She just did not have good reasoning abilities.

She took verses out of the Bible that supported the positions she had already taken in life. And I don't think she ever wanted children. She hated children. She treated her dogs and her plants better than she treated her children. We were in church every time the doors were open. We went to Children's choir and Vacation Bible School. We spent four hours in church every Sunday: two in the morning and two at night. But my mother *never* had a concept of the love of God.

Even though I was hearing the message, the truth in church every Sunday, it was distorted when I got home.

Commandments such as "Children obey your parents," (Ephesians 6:1) became a rationale for the acceptance of incest as well as physical, mental and emotional abuse. Karen's mother turned a blind eye to her husband's sexual abuse of their daughter, hiding behind God's word that the husband is the head of the household and that the wife is to be submissive to him (Ephesians 5:22–24). Karen's parents constantly twisted Scripture to justify the warped lifestyle that was practiced within the walls of their home.

K: Consequently, growing up in sexual abuse, and all of the other dysfunctions in the family, I grew up with such a distorted view of God. It took me most of my young adult life to figure out the truth of Scripture.

Religiosity plagued the Smith's troubled home, confusing Karen for decades to come. James describes God's view on "surface only" or "defiled religion":

If any man among you seem to be religious, and brideleth not his tongue, but deceiveth his own heart, this man's religion is in vain. Pure religion and undefiled before God and the Father is this, To visit the fatherless, and widows in their affliction, and to keep himself unspotted from the world.

James 1:26–27, KJV

Reaching Up for Salvation

But praise God, Karen didn't have to wait that long to begin a personal relationship with her Lord and Savior, Jesus Christ. Even
though she was unable to find Him where He was, He was able to
meet her exactly where she was. As in Bonny's story, when Karen
reached up, the Lord reached down. It happened one sunny spring
day in April of 1960.

> **K:** I was saved when I was nine years old. That was the point where
> I was just going into that normal human growth and development
> stage where my logic was changing. I was beginning to understand
> some abstract things. When the Holy Spirit began to deal with me, I
> had spent the last nine years praying that He would make the abuse
> go away, or make my parents go away, or take me away with Him. I
> prayed every night that I wouldn't wake up in the morning.

So as Karen lay in the grass looking up at the cumulous clouds
floating by, she tried to imagine what Heaven would be like. It was
at that moment that the Holy Spirit beckoned her.

Even though her family's participation in church had been super-
ficial, the seed of the concept of salvation had been planted in Karen.
But there was one very real stumbling block for the abused little
girl: entering into a father-daughter relationship with God. What
should have been a comforting thought was actually a nightmarish
concept to Karen.

> **K:** Because I had been in church, I knew the story of salvation. I
> knew that I was supposed to accept Jesus as my savior–but accepting
> God as a father? To me, God was a "big monster in the sky." I had
> always been taught that God gave us parents to teach us about God.
> So if I had to be abused by my father, then that must mean I would
> be abused by God, the Father, when I got to Heaven. So I didn't
> want to go to Heaven. I really would have preferred going to hell,
> only because I figured that I could bargain with the devil. I knew I
> couldn't bargain with God.
>
> The Holy Spirit dealt with me so deeply that I finally relented.

But I couldn't trust God the Father, I could only trust Jesus. I actually saw Jesus as an abused child, too. My perception, at that time, was that Jesus' Daddy had sent Him down here to get hurt. So I could relate to Jesus as a friend, or "fellow sufferer."

The thought of "God, the Father" was just too scary. So I accepted Christ with the great hope (which, as it turns out, is the truth of scriptures anyway) that Jesus would stand between me and God, and keep God's wrath, or just keep God away from me.

So, with my limited understanding, and with that inability to trust, and all that other stuff that I grew up with, somehow God, in His miraculous way, managed to get through to me. I remember it was such an agonizing decision for me. But God just wouldn't let go of me until I gave my heart to Him.

I was totally alone in the backyard, absolutely miserable, and as soon as I said, "I don't understand it, I don't like it, I'm afraid of you, but I'm going to accept Jesus as my savior," I had an ecstatic joy. And that was a new feeling, because I had never in my life felt happy. I didn't know what that feeling was. I knew it felt wonderful. I didn't even know words to describe it. We didn't have happy words in our vocabulary. We lived with such sorrow and blame and shame and guilt.

That was definitely the greatest experience of my life as far as having a "happy feeling." The only other time I ever felt that way was when my father died because then he would not be a threat to my daughter who was just four months old at the time. I was so relieved that I wouldn't have to worry about him being around her.

Having been fed the hell-fire and brimstone version of the scriptures, Karen had no concept of what Heaven would be like. And even though she didn't completely understand the concept of salvation, she felt in her spirit that it was something she had to do. And as everyone who has experienced the re-birthing process can attest, the first thing the little "new-born" wanted to do, was to tell somebody. This was the greatest moment in her life in terms of experiencing pure, unadulterated joy, and Karen did not have the words to articulate that blessing, or anyone to share it with.

So even though the experience was bitter-sweet, the abused but exceptional child had the wherewithal to turn from her tragic roots and open her heart to the *truth*. In turn, she was blessed with the peace, the joy that surpasses understanding (Philippians 4:7). Salvation was hers in the backyard of the house that held nothing but misery. Praise God!

She had reached out to Christ and He was there. It was a turning point in the young girl's life. The Holy Spirit now lived within her, bringing a conviction and strength that she had never before known.

Because even at the age of ten, Karen sought God's face in terms of needing to know that He thought sexual relations between a father and daughter were wrong. Her twisted upbringing said that God approved. The sick rationale instilled by her mother declared that because God had ordained the man as head of the household, he had God's permission to do whatever he wanted to do, with whomever he wanted to do it with.

But that brainwashing ceased to hold water for Karen after her salvation experience. A supernatural cleansing of her mind and spirit had taken place. And nothing could take that away from her.

> **K:** Instantaneously, when I accepted Christ, I just sort of had this 'knowing" that [the abuse] was *wrong*–my father was wrong. And I shouldn't have to [comply] with him. I also felt guilt, not that I had any choice in letting him [abuse me], but I knew that I had to do whatever I had to do to keep that from happening again. Because I had a sense at that point that it was wrong.

God Provides a Short (But Pivotal) Reprieve

Shortly after she was saved, and as only God could work things out, Karen's father was forced to take a job out of state. During the year that he was gone, the little girl's mind cleared and her logic began to develop. She began to pour over God's word, searching for His position on incest:

> Meanwhile, I had been doing a lot of Bible study and even more

thinking...I decided the games Daddy played were wrong. I had developed a guilty conscience over that, and I promised God I would never let it happen again, no matter what.[4]

Out from under the dark cloud of sexual abuse, the once shy, withdrawn and sickly little girl, began to form a new perspective on life. In fact, when Karen's father returned from his contracted job in New York, it didn't take long for him to realize there was "a new sheriff in town."

K: That was the first time I decided I *wanted* to live. I saw that there *was* hope for a different kind of life. So when he came back, I knew that it was wrong and I wasn't going to let him "do that" to me anymore. The one incident where he tried it again, I hit him over the head with a telephone receiver. I cut his face above his eye. And because he was bleeding and hurting at that point, he just threw me on the ground.

That was the first time I ever *reacted* to anything, other than just being paralyzed, disassociating, and waiting for it to "be over." That was the first time I ever tried to defend myself.

Although Karen's father tried to assault her on several other occasions, she managed to thwart him with a new defiance. Armed with the Holy Ghost and a new sense of self-worth, the once emotionally and mentally paralyzed little girl was now standing up for herself.

From that point on, Karen was determined not to spend another night in the house, vulnerable to her father's advances. As a parent, it's hard to fathom what she decided to do in order to protect herself. At the age of ten, Karen sought refuge from her father by seeking shelter in various other places, depending on the circumstances and the weather. Other safe retreats were found at a sympathizing neighbor's home, abandoned buildings, and a cubby-hole in the basement where the little girl could monitor her father's comings and goings.

When the weather was fair, she would cross a field with waist high weeds to get to a little alcove she had constructed in the woods. This was her sanctuary, her "home away from home."

How sad to know that a little hollow in the woods felt safer to a little girl than did her own bedroom at home. But the good Lord protected her night after night as she slept under the stars.

Where Evil Lurks, Angels Prevail

Day turned to dusk one summer night as Karen made her way across the field. Nearing her wooded "safe house," the little girl heard a car-load of men pull up. It was immediately obvious to Karen that they were a threat.

> **K:** There must have been about six or seven of them. They got out of the car and followed me into the woods. There was *nowhere* for me to go. I had the field on either side, the men behind me, and the woods in front of me. So I was *really stuck.* I started running.
>
> They were following me, and saying things like, "She's mine first." I heard that "zinging" sound as one of the men ripped his belt from his belt loops. Then one of them asked, "What if we get caught?" And one of the guys said, "They'll never find her." So I knew they were planning on raping *and* killing me. And I was *stuck!* I had *nowhere to go!*
>
> I fell on the ground, just paralyzed with fear. And they were all around me. I could see one of the men's shoes through the tall grass. He must have been just a few feet from me. I was just clutching the ground and praying, "Jesus, help me. Jesus, help me." My heart was beating so fast, I thought they'd be able to hear it.
>
> And they kept saying, "Where'd she go?" "Well she was just right here." "She's not getting' away that easy." "She's gotta be here." They were *all* around me. Then the ring-leader of the group said, "*Holy--! What's that?*" And one of them started to scream like he was in agony, as if he was just terrified or shocked. The next thing I knew, they were just pounding the earth, running back to the car.
>
> And I'll never know what happened. But it was almost like they saw something that scared them. And maybe it was just a police car,

but they were exhibiting such terror. Maybe they saw an angel in the sky...I don't know. But God delivered me, because they left.

As soon as I was able to compose myself, I got up. I was so shaky. I was terrified. Not two feet away from me on the path, there was a man's belt. I don't know what those men saw, but I know God protected me.

It was as though the promises found in Psalms 91 were playing out for the little girl who had surrendered her life to Christ. In Him was her fortress. Even though she had not yet received God as her father, she had made a way to His protection through her belief in Christ. God had sent His angel to watch over her, protecting her from all evils of the night. He had shown Himself; he had shown His love to Karen in a mighty way.

> I will say of the Lord, He is my refuge and my fortress: my God; in Him will I trust...He shall cover thee with feathers, and under His wings shalt thou trust: His truth shall be thy shield and buckler. Thou shalt not be afraid for the terror by night; nor for the arrow that flieth by day...A thousand shall fall at thy side, and ten thousand at thy right hand; but it shall not come nigh thee...There shall no evil befall thee...For He shall give his angels charge over thee, to keep thee in all thy ways...Because He hath set his love upon me, therefore will I deliver him: I will set him on high, because he hath known my name. He shall call upon me, and I will answer him: I will be with him in trouble; I will deliver him and honor him. With long life will I satisfy him, and show him my salvation.
>
> Psalm 91: 2, 4–5, 7, 10–11, 14–16, KJV

Seeking God's Character: Battling Fear

Even though she had come to see God as her physical protector, it would be years before Karen would glean any spiritual comfort from the scriptures.

K: It was all about what sorry, low-down scoundrels' people were. There was nothing in the Bible that comforted me.

Sadly enough, however, Karen was unable to seek out God's truth for years later. Reading the Bible was a daunting task—in fact, it was terrifying for the pre-adolescent.

> **K:** Every time the word, "love" was in the bible, I understood that to mean "physical sex." So a lot of the verses that were supposed to be comforting, like, Romans 8:37–39 actually terrified me.
>
> > Nay, in all these things we are more than conquerors through Him that loved us. For I am persuaded, that neither death, nor life, nor angels, nor principalities, nor powers, nor things present, nor things to come, Nor height, nor depth nor any other creature, shall be able to separate us from the love of God, which is in Christ Jesus our Lord. (KJV)
>
> What it said to me was, there was nowhere that I could go and hide from God that he wouldn't find me and do whatever he wanted to do with me.

Although disturbing and sad, the ten-year-old's interpretation was completely understandable considering her abusive background. That, compounded by the fact that all of her biblical teaching up until this time focused on punishment, condemnation verses and a God of wrath instead of a God/Father of love. Karen was growing up in a fog of religious confusion.

During one of his televised broadcast services on TBN, Gregory Dickow [5] discussed the principle of "The Father Fracture" and its devastating effects on a person's ability to trust in God. The Father Fracture involves the fracture of a relationship with one's father, whether through abuse, neglect, or abandonment, etc. The scars from this fracture stay with the affected person throughout their lives, thereby hampering their ability to trust in "God the Father."

Healing that wound can help pave the way to a deeper relationship with the Lord; for we know that the element of trust is crucial to any healthy, meaningful relationship. We are asked to trust with child-like faith (Mark 10:14), but what if our "child within" has been horribly violated by those closest to her?

> **K:** When a child is raised in an environment where they don't want to trust, and they know the world is not a safe place, they can't see God any other way than how they see their earthly parents. My mother thought of Him as a very harsh, punishing God. She never mentioned the love of God. She never understood the salvation story.
>
> I spent my first ten years trying to be good–trying not to make a mistake. Because even though we were taught that we were saved by grace, not by works, my mother would still say things like: "You'll go to hell for lying."
>
> So, even when I tried diligently to read the Bible, to understand God's word, to get closer to Him, Satan used scripture to turn me against God because I didn't understand the *truth* about the scripture. My view of everything was distorted.

Protection Through Childhood and Adolescence

Our ever omnicent God provided Karen with people throughout her life who would offer a safe haven: a peaceful sanctuary away from the insanity of her natural home.

From the age of two, the Jones' house represented Karen's idea of heaven. Two years older than Karen, Janet Jones was the closest thing to a sister that she had. Janet was mentally retarded and physically handicapped, but the two were inseparable throughout childhood. Mr. and Mrs. Jones provided a loving, stable home environment which stood in stark contrast to Karen's home life. Despite her mother's jealousy of the Jones family, Karen managed to find ways to spend as much time as she could at her best friend's house.

Incredibly, Karen never felt drawn to any of the vices of cigarettes, drugs, alcohol or promiscuity during her teen years. She credits God for protecting her from bad habits that were going to be tough to break, or destroy her health.

K: God gave me a certain mindset, or coping skills, which may have included being good, "being a good girl," not doing anything *bad* because I was terrified of God. But still, I think God was protecting me through a lot of things.

At the age of fourteen, Karen took a babysitting job with another one of the families in the neighborhood. The Lord provided just the right refuge at just the right time.

Debbie and Keith had just moved into the neighborhood. Both worked nights and needed someone to care for their three little girls, all under the age of two. For the teenager looking for an escape from an abusive home, it was an "arrangement made in heaven" [6] . The less time she spent at home, the better…especially during the evening hours.

Debbie also arranged for Karen to take a job as a waitress at the restaurant in which she worked. So the self-motivated freshman would leave school, work at the restaurant until 10:00 p.m., and then get to her babysitting job just in time for Debbie to leave for work.

She would spend the next few hours doing homework before the baby would wake for her bottle. Sleep would be had for three or four hours before the baby would wake for the next bottle. After a few more hours of sleep, Karen would wake and get ready for school just in time for Keith to return home from work.

It sounds like a grueling regimen for a fourteen-year-old girl, but Karen even found time on the weekends to look after the little girls who she had fallen in love with. Finding a way to rarely be at home, Karen felt as though she was getting the better end of the deal:

Debbie worried that I wouldn't get enough sleep, knowing at least the youngest one would wake every three or four hours for a bottle. I didn't tell her that three or four hours of uninterrupted sleep was a long time for me. Even when no danger lurked, my fear awakened me every hour or two until now. I felt I should be paying them room and board instead of them paying me for childcare. [7]

Through their cutting comments, Karen's parents let her know that they were less than happy about the new "living arrangement," yet they did not forbid her to continue. So for the next few years, Karen continued on as a "surrogate big sister" to the three little girls.

This safe place that God had provided was most likely key to Karen surviving her teen years with any capacity of mental health. In fact, when Karen eventually married for the first time, Keith, not her father, walked her down the aisle. For obvious reasons, Karen "did not want [her] father to be anywhere *near* the wedding."

A Marriage "Not" Made in Heaven

At the tender age of eighteen, Karen married not for love, but more out of a blind obedience to a passive-aggressive young man. Ted had lived across the street from her from the time she was fourteen years old. Although they never really dated, Ted would profess his undying love for Karen in letters he would write when his family would move out of town from time to time.

Writing from his parent's home in California, Ted, then fifteen, and an eleventh-grade drop-out, declared that he was going to marry Karen one day. A high school freshman, she was nowhere near ready to marry anyone, let alone a boy who she felt absolutely no passion for. But an utter lack of self-esteem and inability to stand up to people, to assert her own needs, left Karen feeling paralyzed and trapped. So much so that she simply went along with the plan for fear of hurting Ted's feelings. She did, however, insist on finishing high school first.

> **K:** I got married at the age of eighteen, but had committed myself to marrying him at the age of fourteen. I idealized everything. I decided that I was going to have this happy little family, and we'll go to church together. Life is going to get better. I just didn't have the reasoning skills at that age to make good decisions.
>
> Because when you get traumatized, you get stuck at the age that the trauma happens. So I was probably an infant in my emotional development. And so I just did what I was told to do.

Karen's lack of enthusiasm for her up-coming wedding competed with the excitement of escaping from her parents and the haunting memories of her home town.

When they did marry in 1967, Ted was stationed in the United States Navy in National City, California.

Both Karen and Ted came from extremely dysfunctional families and consequently their relationship was not a healthy one. Karen describes it as a situation in which she "gave everything and he gave nothing." But moving to the West Coast did provide a great geographic distance between Karen and her painful past, enabling the healing process to gradually begin.

More Meaningful Healing Begins

It wasn't until she was in her mid twenties that Karen was able to even fathom the concept of grace. And, glory to God, she started out by connecting with Jesus. In so doing, she "graduated to seeing the true character of God."

One of the first scriptures she was drawn to was Isaiah 40:31:

> But they that wait upon the Lord shall renew their strength; they shall mount up with wings as eagles; they shall run, and not be weary; and they shall walk, and not faint. (KJV)

K: It meant that I was going to get some control over my life. I was going to be successful over [the abuse].

Karen and Ted moved back to Georgia in 1968. Despite the fact that she was beginning to glean some comfort from the scriptures, Karen's struggle with depression and anxiety attacks continued. As if that wasn't enough, she accidentally discovered that she suffered from D.I.D. (Dissociative Identity Disorder), formerly known as Multiple Personality Disorder. Karen had been attending every seminar she possibly could, trying to figure out what was "wrong" with her. Desperately, she sought out the explanations as to why she wasn't "normal" and making "normal" decisions.

K: I guess I was about thirty when I went to a seminar on Multiple Personality Disorders. And they talked about the different forms of that, like not being able to account for periods of time. And that finally clicked in my mind because all through my childhood, my mother would beat me half to death. And she would say, "I'll teach you to say you hate me! You don't even need to have that word in your vocabulary." And I never remembered telling her that I hated her. I *remember hating her* (laughing), but I don't ever remember *saying it,* because I knew that I'd get killed for it

But apparently the "other me" was very feisty and stuck up for me. And that's the one that she was punishing. By the time she got around to punishing me, the host personality was back in charge— I was so innocent, vulnerable and quiet. I was scared of my own shadow. I would never have dared to talk back to her.

So by the time I got through the Seminar, I thought, "Well, that explains a lot! I just wasn't *present* for half my childhood!"

I mean, people would say things to me like, "I just love the dress you wore to the birthday party yesterday. You looked adorable." And I would think, "Party? What Party?" Or my teachers would say, "Remember class, we talked about 'this or that' last week," and I'd think, "I don't remember talking about that." So I was dissociating. I wasn't even present.

Karen was in her mid thirties (the time when most sexual abuse victims begin to deal with their trauma) when she finally felt "ready and willing" to get help. She recognized that she wasn't "living normally." This included making abnormal decisions in every area of her life including child rearing, spirituality, and not taking care of herself or her husband. Her relationships were failing. Every area of her life was suffering.

K: When I went into counseling, I found out all of the ways that my father's alcoholism had affected my life. I realized for the first time that my mother was mentally ill. I did a lot of growing up. God put a lady in my life that I met through an Incest Survivors group. Just as God would have it and as He designed it, Carolyn lived in my neighborhood. We became best friends and we spent a lot of time searching through the scriptures, asking, "Where *is God* in all of this?" That helped me spiritually more than anything–having a Christian friend who had the same doubts and fears.

The two women poured over Scripture, searching for answers to the questions as to how God can allow incest to happen. Finally they fell upon Leviticus, Chapter 18, which outlines every possible sex act forbidden by God.

> **K:** It mentioned *every possible relationship* (even forbidding sex with animals) *except father-daughter.* And Carolyn and I were both molested by our fathers. And so we asked, "Well, are we just our father's property and God doesn't value us?" But the beginning of [the scriptural discussion] says that no one shall have sexual relations with a close relative:
>
> > None of you shall approach to any that is near of kin to him, to uncover their nakedness; I am the Lord.
> >
> > Leviticus 18:6, KJV
>
> We finally came to the conclusion that, knowing the character of God, He probably didn't find it necessary to say, "Fathers do not sleep with their daughters." That should have been clearly understood because it should be our God-given instinct to *love* our children and not do anything to hurt them. So maybe by *pre-supposition,* God just didn't think he needed to tell us *that.* Because that is definitely covered–there is no closer relation than parent and child.
>
> And maybe that's why God never told us to love our children. He *assumes* we will love our children because *He loves us.* That's what we're supposed to do. Husbands are commanded to love their wives. We're commanded to love each other. We're commanded to love our enemies. But we're never told to love our children, because maybe God assumed that there are some things you just shouldn't have to *tell* people.

Researching God's Truth Re: Incest

Bottom line, the two women *needed to know* that God hated incest.

They *needed to know* that He did not approve of it. They *needed to know* that *they*, not the perpetrator, were in the right. They drew comfort from 2 Samuel 13-19 wherein David's house is throne into utter turmoil after being contaminated by the spirit of incest. Seven chapters are devoted to making it clear that relations between family members are wrong and solicit dire consequences.

And because both women had felt abandoned and betrayed by both parents, they held fast to Psalms 27:10 in which David declares: "When my father and my mother forsake me, then the Lord will take me up." Though Karen and Carolyn had been left with gaping voids in this area of their lives, through His truth, they came to know that God's love was sufficient.

John 10:10 was yet another cornerstone scripture they claimed in their healing process. Though the enemy had lurked about their childhood, "seeking to steal, kill and destroy," the recovering women had discovered the *truth:* Jesus had come "that they might have life, and that they might have it more abundantly" (KJV).

Co-Dependent No More

Another stage in Karen's recovery involved her decision to leave her loveless marriage. For almost twenty years, Karen had put up with a husband who could not provide for his family in any way: economically, emotionally, mentally or spiritually. They were stuck in a stagnant state where neither one was able to grow. As long as Ted failed to provide, and Karen continued to be the enabling all-provider, they were destined to failure.

> **K:** I was so stifled in a marriage that should have never been. Legally we were married, but really we were just polite roommates. I thought he was a Christian, but he wasn't.
>
> It took me twenty years, strictly from a spiritual standpoint to believe that God would not be mad at me if I got a divorce. The more I looked into [God's word], the more I realized what a marriage was, and that was to emotionally support each other. And that wasn't happening. So we never really had a marriage.

It wasn't until Karen left her husband and obtained counseling that she was finally able to mature to the point that she could care for herself and her two daughters; Angela who was eleven, and Maria, age four. It would be a tough road to forge, but for the sake of her mental health and the security of her daughters, Karen found the strength to make the break.

Intuitively she knew it was her responsibility to break the generational curse. It was time for her spirit to be healed so that she could be the mother and the woman that God had predestined her to be. And that was not going to happen in a stifling, co-dependent marriage.

> **K:** I think that's the greatest tragedy [that comes out of abuse] is the spiritual impact. And I think that's why Jesus says, "if anyone should cause a little one to stumble, it would be better that they be cast into the ocean with a millstone about their neck" (Matthew 18:6 paraphrased). And I say this because the only requirement needed to become a Christian is trust. When a child lives in an abusive environment, the first thing it does is destroy that child's ability to trust.
>
> So it took an absolute miracle for God to get through to me when I was nine years old and still living in the abuse.
>
> The other tragedy, other than the spiritual aspect of it, is that it sets you back twenty, thirty, maybe even forty years in your development. There were some things that I just never learned to do, like play, or learning to trust people, or making friends–things that you should learn in pre-school, I didn't learn until I went to counseling in my thirties.

The Haunting Question is Answered:
God's Word Brings Peace

To tell Karen's entire story would require that I devote an entire book to do it justice. But Karen has already done that. The following excerpt from *Blind Trust* will fill in the gaps and reveal the amazing "over-comer" that she is–overcoming the tragic effects of the abuse by turning toward God and his word over and over again.

For decades, Karen's faith had been muted by the nagging question: why does God allow the abuse of innocent children? Finally, one night the overwhelmed single mother lay on her bed crying out to God in frustration. At the time, Karen's best friend, Kelly, a beautiful thirty-one-year-old mother of two lay dying in the hospital from complications with diabetes.

Always the devoted friend and care-giver, Karen was looking after her best friend's two children, her own two kids, and working two jobs. It was at this moment of absolute anguish that the Lord led Karen to the pivotal scripture that would help free her from years of bondage.

> One night, long after the children were in bed, I allowed my pent up emotions to spill. In desperation I cried out to God, "Where are you? And where have you been all my life? If you are [a loving God], and it hurts you to see your children hurt, just where the [heck] were you when I was a little girl and I needed someone to help me? Where are you now when Kelly needs you?" Too angry to do anything but cry, too confused to listen or understand if Christ himself had appeared before me and tried to explain, I spent the next few hours cursing God and venting my frustration any way that happened to strike my fancy as I attempted to clean house and do the laundry.

> A glance at the clock told me it was almost 2:00 a.m. and unfinished chores threatened to eat up the rest of the night...I felt so tired I collapsed into the mountains of socks and underwear that belonged to five different people. Totally spent, I cried some more and begged God to forgive me for my attitude and to assure me of His presence. I needed to know that He does suffer with us, and that He is with us even when we don't feel His presence.

> I was ready now to try to listen to Him. I opened my Living Bible and once again my eyes fell on exactly the message God had for me. In Isaiah 59:15b I read, "The Lord saw all the evil and was displeased to find no steps taken against sin. He saw no one was helping you, and wondered that no one intervened. Therefore he himself stepped in to save you through his mighty power and justice."

Finally! After so many years, I had an answer to my most nagging question. I still don't understand how neighbors, doctors, relatives, pastors, school teachers, and social workers could suspect child abuse and mind their own business. I do know some possible reasons for their human behavior, and I can accept those. What I could not accept was God not intervening. Now I saw that although God's power is not limited, He is dependent on people to physically reach out and touch a child in need of protection.

I thought of my salvation experience at the age of nine, and I realized what an incredible occurrence that was. God had truly intervened. He came to me where I was, because I was unable to come to Him. That He took a child who dared not trust and brought me into a personal relationship with Him is still a miracle beyond my comprehension.

I could clearly see now that when no one else helped, God told me in my spirit to get out of the house at the age of ten. He protected me and guided me in the right paths. The nights I spent in an open field under the stars were not times of danger for me. God lingered alongside me, protecting me from snakes, and men, and the elements. He guided me away from the temptation of drugs and easy money. Instead, he gave me the determination to finish high school and the desire to go to college. He sent good people into my life to counteract the erroneous examples that were there. I looked around at my four-bedroom house. I thought of my children and my friends and I knew He was still blessing me.

I had lived a tragic past, and some of it resulted from my own actions. When I surveyed the tracks of my tears, it seemed incredulous that I, the sweet, good child who grew into a loving, dedicated Christian with extremely high morals and good intentions had, in reality, almost ended my own life, cheated on my husband, had an abortion, and would soon be divorced. I realized that all those things were a natural result of my dysfunctional childhood, and without counseling I would have continued on a self-destructive path. There were many things in my past that brought me shame, but I knew

God had forgiven me. Most importantly, I had forgiven myself. I chose to applaud myself for those accomplishments that deserved a measure of pride.

No one would ever know how hard I worked to overcome my past or just how much courage it took to face each new day. After years of trying, I could now lift my eyes to speak directly with other people, and I could risk disagreeing when necessary. I had never allowed smoking and drinking to become a part of my life, and I respected myself enough to take care of my body. I could even go for simple medical care when needed without assistance. My other personality had integrated. I no longer needed her to cope for me in any everyday situation.

Most importantly, I had broken the cycle of child abuse and learned better parenting skills than the ones my parents modeled for me. I would never be rich or famous or anyone's hero, but I considered myself successful. [8]

What a revelation! Glory to God! How many times does He lead us to *just the right scripture* at *just the right time;* binding up our broken hearts and providing peace for our struggling spirits? Karen had sought the truth "and the truth had set her free" (John 8:32 paraphrased). An integral piece of her recovery that could only have been found by trusting God and seeking His word was finally in place. Triumph over tragedy was in the making!

Onward and Upward With Christ Jesus

Karen would continue her counseling for several years. Finally, armed with a new sense of direction, confidence and maturity, the thirty-eight-year-old divorced mother of two signed up for classes at a local university. She eventually transferred to a Theological Seminary where she obtained a B.A. and Masters in Psychology and Christian counseling.

This achievement would be highly commendable on its face, but for a recovering abuse victim, it was almost miraculous. Karen had clung to God and involved Him in her ambitions for a career. The result was another triumph over her tragedy.

> **K:** The first test I took in college I got a *ninety-eight!* I kept that score sheet and put it in a scrapbook as a reminder that "*I am not stupid.*"
>
> My mother always told me I was stupid, that college wasn't for women, that nobody wanted to hear what I had to say, that it was okay if I had an opinion as long as I kept it to myself. (Laughing) I think it's kind of ironic now that people *pay me* to get my opinion!

Today: Living a Victorious Life

For the past four years, Karen has specialized in trauma in both adults and children. She also treats children of divorce, Katrina victims, sexual abuse, and any kind of self-injury. Her choice of career and the publishing of her book, *Blind Trust,* are both testimonies to her dedication to turning the effects of her own tragedy into an opportunity to help others. Once again, Satan is defeated and "in all things God works for the good of those who love Him, who have been called according to His purpose" (Romans 8:28, NIV). Halleluiah!

In 1999, Karen married, Jim, a man who is equally yoked to her in every way. The recipient of a Seminary Doctorate Degree, Jim has just been commissioned to start up a Single's Group at the church he and Karen attend. In fact, the couple met in church while attending Sunday school.

> **K:** Simply put, I see Jesus through Jim. He is such a Godly man. I am so blessed to have him in my life. He is the kind of husband that God intended every man to be. He is so giving. In fact, he just can't give enough. Whatever it takes to help someone, he's always there. He is just a good guy.

Karen's eldest daughter, Angela, is now thirty-one. She is married, has four children and lives in Florida. Maria, age twenty-four, lives in Georgia with her husband and two children. She is an eighth grade teacher and has a special gift for communicating with pre-teens: brave girl!

As mentioned earlier, Karen's father died when she was twenty-four and her eldest daughter, Angela, was four months old. As Karen said, it was one of the most joyous moments of her life because it meant that her daughter would not be endangered. Not surprisingly, Lester Smith was just forty-nine when he succumbed to the effects of cirrhosis of the liver.

It had been ten years since Karen had had any contact with her father because he was "just too dangerous." However, she felt obliged to maintain contact and care for her mother her when needed. Rose died at the age of seventy-four.

At least from all outward indications, Karen and her brother, Randy, seem to have fared the best in terms of the lasting effects of abuse. In *Blind Trust,* Karen describes her brother as the "clown" of the family, the child who scoffed at danger…and that…because Randy suffered the least abuse and because of his personality type, circumstances place him as the most likely to succeed"[9] (208). He has been happily married to the same woman since the age of seventeen and they have raised three children.

Finding a "legal and acceptable way to confront the drunks and abusive members of society"[9] (208), Randy has dedicated his life to law enforcement, and skydives for fun. Although Karen and Randy live less than ten miles apart, they rarely speak or visit. However, they do have an unspoken respect and love for each other that allow them to call on each other in time of need.

Unfortunately, Karen's oldest and the youngest brothers did not weather the storm quite as well. She believes the first-born, Micah, suffers from delusions of grandeur and paranoia. The youngest, Jeff, was unable to escape from his mother's domination, has fought the battle with drugs and alcohol, and continues to live as a recluse.

Clearly, the fall-out from severe childhood abuse leaves devastation in its wake—but it's a devastation that can be overcome by reaching toward our Heavenly Father and unraveling the trauma with a qualified, compassionate therapist.

A Final Comment From Karen:

K: Maya Angelou says in one of her books, that "the greatest need a lonely child has is the unshaking need for an unshakeable God." I think that pretty much sums up my childhood. The only thing that kept me going was the hope that God thought [the incest] was wrong and that God was my deliverer from it. And He *did* deliver me from it.

And He protected me–as much physical abuse as there was, I never had any broken bones.

I still don't have the answers within myself as to why God allows children to be abused. I mean, I understand it from a philosophical standpoint, of how we have the choice of either making something out of our past, or we being overtaken by it. But I still don't have the answer to that spiritual question, "Why does God allow innocent children to suffer?"

The final words from *Blind Trust* illustrate what the end result can be: who we can become, and what we can offer to others when we apply God's word to the tragedies we face. The unmistakable triumph of the human spirit and the resulting vision are found in the last fifteen lines of the epilogue:

My *dream* is that someday there will be medical doctors who are trained in Post-Traumatic Stress Disorder, and who are willing to work with patients to negotiate the best health care for those afflicted.

My *hope* is that we will all do our part to prevent abuse in any form and that we will lessen the aftermath for survivors by being more understanding and less judgmental of each other.

My *mission* is to be the best that I can be, because I believe when we better ourselves we better those around us.

My *prayer* is that victims will find comfort in the love and caring of others, and that through our mutual support we will all find the world a safer, kinder place.

To those who struggle with the shackles of their past and to their loved ones who live in its shadow, may your courage be rewarded with peace and your lives be blessed with joy. [10]

Amen, girlfriend, amen.

Additional Scripture

Theme: God condemns incest and sexual sin (and issues severe punishment).
Leviticus 20:11, 12, 17, 19–21
Deuteronomy 22:30, 27:20–23
Ezekiel 22:11

Theme: immoral hypocrites
1 Corinthians 5: 1, 9–13 (KJV, LASB)

Paul calls on the Corinthian Church to expel the immoral hypocrites who rationalize their wickedness, sexually immoral behavior, drunkenness, slanderous speech, greediness, idol worship and swindling.

Theme: battling evil and the sin of the world
Romans 12:21 (KJV, LASB)
"Be not overcome of evil, but overcome evil with good."
Romans 12:2 (KJV, LASB)
"And be not conformed to this world: but be ye transformed by the renewing of your mind, that ye may prove what is that good, and acceptable, and perfect, will of God."

Theme: God's protection in the midst of danger
Psalm 91 in its entirety (KJV, LASB)
God doesn't promise a world free from danger, but he does promise his help whenever we face danger.

*Special note from the author:

I strongly urge any Christian woman who is considering counseling, to seek out a professional Christian counselor. Because our faith is so ingrained in our mindset and the way we approach life, I believe it's absolutely vital to the success of the counseling, that the counselor approach the treatment from a Biblical as well as psychological perspective.

RESOURCES

(Taken from *Blind Trust*)
Austin, Karen. *Blind Trust: a child's legacy.* Kennesaw: Crossroads Counseling, 1999.

To obtain a copy of *Blind Trust*, write to:
Crossroads Counseling
1301 Shiloh Rd., Suite 610
Kennesaw, GA, 30144

VIDEOS

What Do I Say Now?
Committee for Children
To order: 1–800–634–4449
*Teaches parents how to talk to their children in non-threatening ways about how to protect oneself from abuse.

Break the Silence: Kids Against Abuse
Arnold Shapiro Productions (1994)
Most appropriate for ages 8–15
*Excellent video for explaining different forms of child abuse and how children have coped with and healed from abuse.

Hear Their Cries: Religious Responses to Child Abuse

Not In My Church, Not In My Congregation
Center for the Prevention of Sexual and Domestic Violence (1991)
To order: (206) 634–1903
*older teens and adults

Identifying, Reporting & Handling Disclosure of Sexually Abused Children
Committee for Children (1988)
*Target audience: School teachers and personnel

Scared Silent: Exposing and Ending Child Abuse
Arnold Shapiro Productions (1992)
Hosted by Oprah Winfrey
*older teens and adults

BOOKS FOR ADULT SURVIVORS

Incest and Sexuality: A Guide to Understanding and Healing
W. Maltz and B. Holdman (1987)
Lexington Books: New York *ISBN 0–669–14085–6

Secret Survivors: Uncovering Incest and Its Aftereffects in Women
E. Sue Blume (1990)
John Wiley and Son's Pub. *ISBN 0–471–61843–8

United We Stand: A Book for People with Multiple Personalities
Eliana Gil (1990)
Launch Press: Walnut Creek, CA

Victims No Longer
Mike Lew (1990)
Harper & Row: New York *ISBN 0–06–097300–5, PL
*for male victims of sexual abuse

Women Who Hurt Themselves: A Book of Hope & Understanding
Dusty Miller (1995)
Basic ISBN 0–465–09219–5

Can I Look Now: Recovering From Multiple Personality Disorder
M. Evers-Szostak and S. Sanders
R. Downing

FOR PARENTS, PARTNERS AND OTHER FAMILY MEMBERS OF SURVIVORS

Abused Boys: The Neglected Victims of Sexual Abuse
M. Hunter (1991)
Fawcett *ISBN 0-449-90629-9

Allies in Healing: When the Person You Love Was Sexually Abused As a Child
Laura Davis (1991)
Harper Collins Publisher: New York *ISBN 0-06-096883-4

If She is Raped: A Guidebook for Husbands, Fathers, and Male Friends
Alan McEvoy and Jeff Brookings (1991)
*older teens and adult males

Outgrowing the Pain Together: A Book for Spouses and Partners of Adults Abused As Children
Eliana Gil: (1992)
New York *ISBN 0-440-50372-8

When the Bough Breaks: A Helping Guide for Parents of Sexually Abused Children
Aphrodite Matsakies
New Harbinger Press

Reflections

Chapter 5

Bonny's Story
The Steps of a Righteous Man [Or Woman] Are Ordered
(Psalm 37:23–25)

"...I will never leave you, nor forsake you."

Joshua 1:5b (NIV)

In high school...I died.

In the eleventh grade I got alcohol poisoning at a football game. And [the doctors] also thought that there was something laced into what I was drinking because I shouldn't have had the extreme reaction that I did.

My heart stopped beating three times. They declared me legally dead in the Emergency Room.

Bonny

[The] near-death experience would change her life forever. Despite her youthful antics, she knew the Lord at this time. She remembered the saying, "If you reach up, Jesus will reach down the rest of the way."

The Interview

When I met with Bonny at a restaurant close to her office, I knew who she was the instant I saw her. She is just one of those people who you look at and say, "*That's* what I want. That's the level of faith and energy that I want to aspire to." Bonny *has it*. She has the faith that jumps out at you, whether you're ready for it or not. And she's bold in her presentation of the Gospel. Despite her difficult circumstances, s*he is on fire*.

The forty-two-year-old suffers from debilitating back pain, but you would never know it. We sat at lunch for three hours, conducting the taped interview and sharing in fellowship. If you have ever suffered from back pain, you know how uncomfortable it is to sit for any length of time. But we had such a refreshing, joyous, and often humorous, time in the Lord. Her smile never broke, her spirit-filled countenance never faltered, she never once complained.

As she relayed her story, it was clear: Romans 8:28 is the cornerstone scripture for Bonny's 3T Vision.

> And we know that all things work together for good to them that love God, to them who are the called according to his purpose. (KJV)

Claiming this verse and applying it, time and again, she has triumphed over every tragedy that has come her way.

After wrapping up the interview, we "hobbled" out of the restaurant and onto the street. As Bonny returned to work, and I to the parking deck, my new-found friend praised the Lord the whole way for an awesome time of fellowship. She had quite a walk back to the office, but her chin was up, her back was straight, and she claimed a complete healing for the both of us as we parted ways. That's Bonny, and this is her story:

B: *There are two things that I want to stress here. One of them is that through everything, and even up until this day, I have always had an unexplained peace that everything's going to be okay. It's subconscious.*

The second is that, from a very young age, I've always felt that God's hand was on me. It always reminds me of the scripture from Jeremiah: "Before I formed you in the womb I knew you, before you were born I set you apart;" (Jeremiah 1:5, NIV).

It's only been in the last several years that I've realized how in control God is in everything. You know, "The steps of the good [righteous] man are ordered by the Lord: and He delighteth in his way" (Psalm 37:23, KJV). To know that is so freeing.

Let the Little Children Come

And he took them up into his arms, put his hands upon them, and blessed them.

Mark 10:16, KJV

I am your Creator. You were in my care even before you were born.

Isaiah 44:2, *CEV*

Even before she knew Jesus as her savior, Bonny sensed His presence in her life.

B: [Jesus] took the time to come to me in a dream. He let me know that everything was going to be okay, because things weren't very good at the house.

Growing up in a small town just south-west of Atlanta, GA, the fifth-grader was not living the all-American, *Beaver Cleaver* childhood. Instead she was the child of an alcoholic mother, and a kind, but enabling, father.

B: I'm not saying it was always bad. We had some challenging times, but we had some good times, too. I was adopted. So I thank God I wasn't aborted. I thank my birth mother for not doing that. And I know that I was exactly where I was supposed to be. I love my parents.

But my mother was very cold and shut down emotionally. She could be mean and cutting. Really, the only time she showed affection was when she was drinking; and it didn't always happen then. And she was the disciplinarian. She was a perfectionist and worked us hard around the house. That was good in a way because it instilled in us a great work ethic. But one of the things that really bothered me was the way she would do something for somebody and then turn around and complain about it. She was a self-absorbed, addictive personality.

Dad, on the other hand, was the classic enabler. He was the man who went to work, watched cartoons with us and read the paper. He was a caring man; he would give you the shirt off of his back. But he was emotionally shut down, too.

As in Karen's story, our gracious and merciful Lord saw a child in trouble and began to intervene in the youngster's life. He strategically placed strong believers in Bonny's path, providing her with Godly examples of what it was like to be part of a Christian home. Because of this, the young girl could see how healthy married couples were supposed to interact and treat each other. One of these families lived next door to Bonny.

B: The Shipleys were our next door neighbors and I was best friends with their daughter, Katie. We are the same age, in fact, our birthdays are just weeks apart. The Shipleys had married later in life and were in their late thirties before they had children. But what really stands out in my mind is how much they *talked.* Unlike my own family, they talked around the dinner table, they just talked and talked. I always looked forward to spending time around their dinner table. And they gave glory to God in *everything.*

Bonny was also acutely aware that despite the fact that the Shipleys were a one-income household, the Lord not only provided for them, He blessed them abundantly. They were the perfect illustration of the truth that as long as we keep the Lord first in our lives, He will give us everything we need and then some.

But seek ye first the kingdom of God, and his righteousness; and all these things shall be added unto you.

Matthew 6:33, KJV

B: Mrs. Shipley was a homemaker and Mr. Shipley was the sole breadwinner. He was a school teacher, so it's pretty safe to say he made a modest an income. But they tithed and were faithful to the Lord. And they were able to take a vacation every year. They were always provided for.

In contrast, both of my parents worked, but we never had enough money. During my entire childhood, we went to Florida twice.

We went to church regularly, but both of my parents drank. My mother was a pianist at our Baptist church, but behind closed doors she disrupted our family life. She was in and out of rehab centers.

My senior year of high school was particularly stressful. She would disappear for days at a time. Then she would show up at midnight and sit in the kitchen, eating a box of fried chicken. Or she would flick all of our lights on in the middle of the night, and demand that we all talk to her until the early morning hours.

I can remember one time she fell asleep on the couch (while drinking) and smoking a cigarette. I could smell the smoke as I was coming home from school. The couch had caught on fire. Mrs. Shipley helped me drag both my mother and the couch outside where we proceeded to hose them down...Always to my rescue were the Shipleys.

Bonny chuckles heartily while revealing this memory, but you can hear that subtle twinge of pain that she has trained herself to deflect with humor.

But God is faithful. During those years, He provided Bonny with exposure to yet another Christian family who were also instrumental in influencing her early Christian walk. The Howards were friends of the Shipleys and when the two families got together, Bonny was able to see how two loving Christian families interacted.

B: They showed affection to each other. They walked the walk. I was able to spend time at the Howard's home as well. They talked about the Bible. They boldly talked about Christ within the house and with others. That made a big difference to me as I share my faith with people today.

Salvation: Spiritual and Physical

And, glory to God, the Christian seed that the Lord provided came to fruition in the summer of 1976. The twelve-year-old was attending a youth retreat at Tacoa Bible College in Tacoa, GA.

> **B:** It was a Sunday morning. I woke up feeling so emotional. We had had an awesome service the night before. It was as though my senses had been awakened to God's creation: the grass was greener; the sky was bluer. The people at the retreat sensed that something was going on with me. As I was talking to them, I accepted Christ.
>
> When my Dad came to pick me up, the Youth Leader leaned into the car window and told him that I had accepted Christ. We went to church later that night. I went up to the alter during alter call and turned my life over to Christ. I remember the song, *I Surrender All* was playing.

Both her salvation and the Lord's promise to her that everything was going to be okay got Bonny through to high school. It was in her junior year that the damage from living in an alcoholic home began to manifest itself and become apparent. She began to dabble in witchcraft, which, she says, "gave Satan an opening to her mind." She also began to flirt with alcohol. The wheels were falling off. Bonny describes the horrific turning point with her characteristic use of dark humor:

> **B:** Then in high school...I died.
>
> In the eleventh grade I got alcohol poisoning at a football game. And [the doctors] also thought that there was something laced into what I was drinking because I shouldn't have had the extreme reaction that I did.
>
> The girl that I was with dumped me off at my house on the sidewalk. And, you know, she took a lot of persecution for that, but I don't know what I would have done in that situation. She was just sixteen years old!

Thank God, one of Bonny's neighbors saw what was going on

and knocked on her parent's door. Praise God, again, Bonny's mother happened to be in a sober period of her life. She knew enough to turn her daughter over on her side to prevent her from aspirating the vomit into her lungs. But the harrowing experience was just beginning.

B: My heart stopped beating three times. They declared me legally dead in the Emergency Room.

The near-death experience would change Bonny's life forever. Despite her youthful antics, she knew the Lord at this time. She remembered the saying, "If you reach up, Jesus will reach down the rest of the way." This promise is based on the scripture mentioned previously that if we call out to God, He is faithful to answer us:

"Because He hath set his love upon me, therefore will I deliver him: I will set him on high, because he hath known my name. He shall call upon me, and I will answer him: I will be with him in trouble; I will deliver him and honor him. With long life will I satisfy him, and show him my salvation."

Psalms 91: 14–16, KJV

B: I was reaching up to him in this dream, and our fingers touched. And I said, "I want to come home." There was all this light everywhere. And the way He smiled at me…I'll never forget it. And he said, "You can't. You're not done yet."

That was when I woke up in the E.R. I remember waking up and seeing the doctors and nurses to the side of me. I asked them, "What's going on?" And they were all so shocked to see me: the doctors, the nurses and my parents.

Some of the students at her high school were in for the shock of their lives as well…An EMT volunteer who went to school with Bonny had already told everyone that she was dead! You can imagine the commotion she caused when she returned to school on Monday: like Lazarus, it was as if she had literally risen from the dead!

As God always does, he transformed this tragic, alcohol-related incident into a blessing for Bonny's family (Romans 8:28). This family desperately needed to confront the issue of alcoholism in an open and honest dialogue. Her almost fatal experience turned out to be the catalyst for this discussion which *then* led to a conversation about *salvation*. During this rare meaningful exchange between Bonny and her parents, she discovered that her mother was saved, but her father wasn't.

> **B:** He was a good person, he *is* a good person. But goodness doesn't get you into heaven. He totally enabled my mother. They were still married when I graduated from high school.

After she graduated from high school in 1981, Bonny felt compelled to get as far away from her mother as possible. Sadly, her mother would continue her rehab revolving door policy for the next several years. The two ended up being estranged for about six years.

> **B:** She was everything I wasn't going to be.

During that year away from home, Christ was not a priority in Bonny's life. She went to live in Newnan, GA, and worked at a drug store for a while. When she took a different job closer to her hometown, the commute made less and less sense.

Moving back in with her mother and father was not an option. Instead, she moved in with the Shipleys who still lived next door-of course, that decision did not sit well with Bonny's parents.

> **B:** Instead of dealing with the problem, it was all about, "What would the neighbors think?"

Undeterred, Bonny lived with the Shipleys for about a year. During that time, she was able to get back into church regularly, making Christ her focal point once again.

Soul Mates Stand Strong

On March 31, 1982, the eighteen-year-old met her soul-mate and future husband, Luke. The two almost never met. But, as always,

God had a plan. Bonny's friends had gone skating and had not invited her. Despite being slighted, she called up another girlfriend, and the two set off for the skating rink.

> **B:** I may never have met Luke that night, but it didn't matter because "all of my steps are ordered" (Psalms 37:23–25). We were supposed to meet. I was playing the field at that time, but the moment I saw Luke, I told my girlfriend that I was going to marry him.

The two hit it off from the very beginning. Sitting in the bleachers, they stayed up all night together, talking. It wasn't long before they discovered how much they had in common. Both Luke and Bonny were adopted and both had dealt with "challenging family lives." They were inseparable from that point on, and were married the following year.

Unfortunately, one of the many things that Bonny and Luke had in common as teenagers was an interest in the occult. However, in the late 1980's, the couple turned their lives back to the Lord. They had made their decision plain through their dedication to the Word and heavy involvement in their church.

And we all know what happens as we grow closer to the Lord.... Satan sits up and takes notice. There's a saying, "If Satan's not after you, you're not living for the Lord." Well...he was coming after Bonny and Luke with a vengeance. The fight was on. The couple had re-entered into the Christ-centered spirit realm where we "wrestle not against flesh and blood," but against powers, principalities and "spiritual wickedness in high places" (Ephesians 6:12). They would have to "put on the whole armour of God" if they were going to survive the onslaught of the enemy's attacks (Ephesians 6:13)

> **B:** [Satan] started coming to me in dreams, flooding me with lies, telling me I was going to be his. I continually told him that I was not going to be his; that I was covered in the blood. I was with Jesus, and my decision was clear.
>
> But there was this one night when we were living with Luke's mother. We were all asleep in our beds. I was sleeping on the side of the bed closest to the bathroom. I woke up and heard all kinds of

noise and saw lights flashing. I looked up *and there was a steam roller coming out of the bathroom!* It was about to roll over us, so I put my hand out. And I had scrapes all over my hand!

[With my other hand] I was pushing Luke out of the bed and screaming at the top of my lungs. Luke didn't see anything, so he was yelling, "What? What?" And I asked, "Don't you see it? It's a steam roller!" That's when my mother-in-law came to the door and that's what broke the vision. To me, that was the enemy trying to kill [our spirit] because we were so active in the Church.

Everyone finally settled down and went back to sleep, but the enemy wasn't finished. However, this time, Bonny was not alone in her perception. She awoke to feel and see something sitting on her chest. She could not breathe. Bonny reached up and grabbed her husband's arm. And this time, he sensed the presence of [the demon spirit] too.

B: We immediately started praying in tongues against the spirit, and it finally left. Luke later said that he did not think one of us was going to make it through the night, but glory to God, we did. He delivered us from all of that.

But we know how persistent the enemy can be, especially when it comes to married couples who have a special calling on them to serve the Lord. Marital problems were looming just around the corner.

What followed was a somewhat bizarre turn of events. After eight years of marriage, Luke decided that he wanted to cut ties with Bonny and their family in North Georgia to build a life with his biological family in South Georgia.

Ironically, Luke told his wife of his plans to divorce her on *Mother's Day* of 1991. The divorce was final that August. But Praise God, the Holy Spirit would step in to restore their relationship and... ready for this? They were *remarried* in February of 1993!

B: A lot of our problems stemmed from Luke's low self-esteem. We broke up when his birth-mother came on the scene. But I just never felt like we were always going to be apart because we had such a connection. And looking back now, I can see how the Lord worked through all of the problems and just always kept us connected.

During the process of reconciliation, Bonny had reservations. Understandably, she "did not want to go through that rejection again." Desiring to "have God's will in [her] life," Bonny consulted one of her associate pastors.

B: I knew that if I didn't stay on the path that I felt like God wanted us on, then I would really lose some blessings. I knew our life would never be like it should be.

Despite the couple's counseling, Bonny continued to struggle with the old, "Should I or shouldn't I?" Her deep-seeded fear of rejection challenged her ability to hear from God. Then God provided a break-through for her. He sent a word of prophecy (we know how powerful that can be), and delivered her from fear.

B: During one of the sermons, the senior pastor gave me and Luke a word of prophecy that would be instrumental in my life. He basically told us that the Lord was going to restore what had happened to us, that he was going to use us. He wasn't sure exactly how God was going to use us, but it would be in a way that would fulfill His will in this mission. He began with:

"The Lord would say, 'My times for refreshing are always for the restitution and restoration of all things. I say to you this day to know that by my Spirit, I can and I will restore all in your life. I speak faith to you, I speak hope to you, I speak my love to you. I let you know this moment, in this time, in this hour that My Spirit is among you and My Spirit is there to help you and to strengthen you. I speak a word of encouragement to you this day to know that all that is involved, all that the enemy has taken, all that even the years the cankerworm has eaten away, I the Lord, by My Spirit, will bring about the restoration of all things unto you, says the Spirit of the Lord."

As I was rejoicing and claiming those words for me and Luke, the
pastor turned toward the section we were in and pointed to us. It was
a very large church. He didn't know us from the man in the moon.
But God did. The pastor continued:

"The Lord wants you to know that "All is well." There is some
release in the Spirit that God is bringing you both in to. And
there are some people that He wants you to be an influence
upon. I don't know if He wants you to bring them into the
Kingdom or bring enlightenment to them, but the Lord is
going to give you the wisdom and the anointing and the timing
to minister God's grace to those people. You've got a real heart
for others and that's a gift of the Lord. It's a true love for others
that God has given you, and you're going to be able to reach
out to those others with wisdom and understanding. But the
most important thing is that you have the love to reach out to
others, and God's going to bless you as you go. You'll go in the
might and in the power of the Spirit to minister God's grace
and mercy to those people. Amen."

This was so exciting for me. It confirmed to me that Luke and I
should be together.

Bonny's fear instantly dissipated. As we've seen before, and as it
is written, *true* prophecy delivers the strength, courage and comfort
that we need to continue forward (1 Corinthians 14:31). But we must
make that decision to hold onto that *truth,* that word from God.
That's the only way we can claim the *triumph* over the brokenness in
our lives, and move on, fulfilling God's *vision,* his plan, his purpose
for our lives. As long as we hang on to that fear, we are of no use to
God, ourselves, or others. Put simply: we're stuck.

But Bonny was no longer in limbo. She took this prophecy to
heart, received the blessings and reclaimed her 3T Vision! Halleluiah! The brokenness was restored. As mentioned before, Luke and
Bonny were remarried in February of 1993.

Unity is Challenged Again

For the next seven years, they enjoyed a stable married life. But the enemy came knocking once again. By this time, he had learned that he couldn't take Bonny down directly. The next best thing, the thing that would hurt and disrupt her life the most, would be to pursue Luke instead.

Sure enough, during the spring of 2000, Bonny began to notice changes in her husband, both physically and behaviorally. Being naïve about the drug world, she could never have fathomed the sort of darkness her husband had embraced.

> **B:** At first, I just knew he was losing weight and he wasn't around the house much. Then he disappeared for nine days, and it was just awful.
>
> Finally after six weeks of this, he came to me and he told me that he was using crack cocaine.
>
> I just cried out to the Lord. I asked him, "Why is this happening?"
>
> Many of my friends told me that I should just leave him. But I never did get a peace about that because I had this promise [from the pastor] from August of 1991. And when God gives you a promise, you hold onto it.
>
> The enemy knew he couldn't have me. And I wasn't going to let him have Luke either.

Luke would continue the all-too familiar cycle of on again, off again, drug use for the next three years. Bonny refused to enable her husband, but at the same time, she refused to give up. She continued to pray. The day of reckoning did not come until June 12th of 2003. Luke had fallen off the wagon after being clean for ten months.

> **B:** I was supposed to go to Miami on a girl's trip. It was a Thursday night and I had gone to bed because Luke wasn't in yet. He had told me he was working late, but he wasn't. I woke up about 3 a.m. Luke was gone and so was his truck. I was just devastated because he had been sober for over ten months.

When he finally called later that morning, I said, "Don't you think you need to come home?"

But before Luke came home, I came up with a list of six things that he had to do that were non-negotiable, or he couldn't stay [at home]: he had to give me all of his money; he couldn't have access to any money—he had to give every bit of it to me and show me the check stubs; he had to attend Narcotics Anonymous meetings; we had to get involved in church again; we had to attend Christian marriage counseling; and *he could not tell me one more lie.*

Bonny had reached the end of her "faithful, supportive Christian wife" rope. Enough had been enough. When he did arrive home at about noon that day, her anger and hurt got the better of her.

B: I'll never forget when he came in and he walked up to me, I was so mad at him. I hit him as hard as I could. I asked him, "*How could you do this?* God has spared you again. Now what are you going to do with it?"

God had saved his life so many times. And at the time we were going through it, I kept asking myself, "What lesson is God trying to teach him? But it turned out that God wasn't trying to teach Luke a lesson, it was *my lesson,* too! And Lord, it was a lesson learned!

And the lesson was that *I can do nothing on my own,* that *prayer changes things.* It sure changed me. And, as it turned out, the Lord was preparing us both for the battles that only *He* could know were coming up. During that time, I clung to the promise that:

"…the sufferings of this present time are not worthy to be compared with the glory which shall be revealed in us."

Romans 8:18, KJV

Luke agreed to five of the six conditions: he had attended NA meetings in the past, and had found them to be counter-productive. His experience had been that because the meetings focused the conversation on using drugs, it was more apt to tempt him to use again.

After discussing it with the counselor, they all agreed that putting the NA meetings on the back burner at that time would be okay as long as he attended the marriage counseling. The couple benefited greatly from one-on-one and couple's counseling.

> **B:** That was one of the best things that we ever did. Our Christian counselor taught us *how* to argue. She showed us how to be as man and wife. After many stops and starts, by the grace of God, Luke finally came clean. It was June 14, 2003. We were over $30,000 in debt, but his life had been spared and we had each other.
>
> But more than that, we had God. We were at Mountain View Baptist Church the following Sunday. Because I knew that it was all in vain if we didn't put God first in our lives. In July of 2005, he was delivered of depression and smoking (which he had picked up in 1999). *Praise to God!* Because God is the *only one* who could have delivered Luke from his over three-pack per day habit, enabling him to quit cold-turkey.
>
> And here we are! To make a long story short, Luke has been clean for three years. And all of this has made us stronger, because we've learned to keep our focus on the Lord. Having gone through those battles we learned to *stand strong,* putting on the whole armor of God (Ephesians 6:11–13). We learned to see with "spiritual eyes" and not in the natural.

Bonny and Luke were going to need all the strength they could get from the Lord in order to triumph over the warfare they would encounter over the next couple of years.

The Issue of Blood (Feb. 2004)

During most of Bonny's married life, she had experienced severe pelvic bleeding. Everyone in her life attributed it to being over-weight, or being over thirty. Knowing instinctively that something was wrong, she sought a new gynecologist. She was "sick to death of the bleeding" and finally decided to have a hysterectomy.

Once again, God's hand was on her during the preparation and the surgery. It turned out that Bonny had one of the worst cases of endometriosis that the doctor had ever seen. Were it not for God's intervention at this stage, she believes she would not be here today. Here's what happened:

> **B:** They *could not* get the I.V. (intravenous line) in me. They even called the head of anesthesiology. Between the Lanacain (to numb the injection sites) and the actual attempts to run an I.V., they poked me over *sixty times*. They even tried my feet.

By this time, Bonny was a human pin cushion. The nurses explained to Bonny, when an I.V. cannot be run conventionally, the patient can be taken into the operating room and put to sleep. The hope is that the veins will then pop up, making it easier to find a good one.

> **B:** So they put me in [the operating room] and they put me to sleep. And as they were getting me ready, my doctor said he was looking at my abdominal area and something didn't look right. So he felt around and he said it was kind of lopsided. Instead of doing the Caesarian cut, he went up my stomach and around my belly button. Had he gone in with the Caesarian cut, I would have ended up with an anchor cut which would have been more painful and difficult to heal.

Bonny's doctor later told her that when he made the incision and got a good look at the situation, he was devastated. The endometriosis had spread like wild fire. Her ovaries were full of it, her bladder was adhered to her pelvic wall and adhesions were everywhere. The disease had also spread to Bonny's bowels, kidneys, and urinary tract. The surgeon knew immediately that he had to have help. And once again, God provided.

> **B:** He called down to the E.R. because he had never done anything this extensive. And the only doctor down there was an *urologist*— *ex*actly what he needed, because that system is so delicate.

Now tell me *that's* not a "God thing!" Praise Jesus, Bonny came through the surgery and was taken back up to her room. Because of the extensive nature of the surgery, "the jury was out" as to whether she would ever have proper use of her urological system again. This information was initially kept from her, so as not to alarm her in the initial stages of healing. What happened next is yet another piece of dark comedy "a la Bonny."

> **B:** Over the next day or two, they removed the catheter. I went into the bathroom, and I was "doing my thing," when all of a sudden, I hear everyone outside the door praising the Lord! And that's when they told me how extensive the damage was.

It would be months before she would fully recover…However, the next attack was right around the corner. But…Glory to God…3T Vision would prevail.

Jesus "Had Her Back"

For years, Bonny had rebuked her nagging back pain, but eventually, the pain become unbearable. In April of 2005, she was diagnosed with a bulging disc.

> **B:** I had a piercing pain in my left side that went all the way down to my knee. Chiropractic helped, but then we got busy with moving to Griffen and the pain just got worse.
>
> Later that year, in November, I was walking across the skywalk to my office, when the pain was so bad it forced me to turn to the side. An MRI (magnetic resonance image) later revealed that I had torn the disc.
>
> Then during Thanksgiving weekend, I overdid it. I was making my bed on the Friday morning when the disc finally *cracked*. It was actually *sitting* on my spinal cord. You want to talk about excruciating pain!

Once again, Luke and Bonny were rewarded for their faithfulness. The Lord would provide everything they needed during yet another season of tragedy.

The Potter Shapes His Saints

> **B:** Had [my back injury] happened before we moved, we wouldn't

have had the help we had. As it turned out, we had our church family. They were there, they took care of us, and they really ministered to Luke. And that was the main thing, because after that, he really came out of his shell–he became the husband that he should be.

During the hysterectomy and the procedures leading up to it, Luke had kept his distance. He had never liked hospitals (who does?) and allowed that phobia to dictate his level of support. But because he had the support of his church family during this next surgery, he responded as a Godly husband, never leaving his wife's side for a moment.

Truth had triumphed over a weakness in Luke's character. It would mean all the difference in how this couple would work together to triumph over yet another tragedy. It's just another example of the spiritual boost we receive when fellow Christians agree with us, lifting us up in times of trouble (Matthew 18:19–20).

Luke and Bonny were going to need all of the love and support they could get. The back surgery proved to be more extensive than what they had expected. A few nights after the surgery, Bonny woke up to an excruciating pain that began at the surgical site and emanated down both legs.

> **B:** [The spasm] would fill up one leg to the point that I was screaming in pain. While it was still throbbing, [the spasm] would go down the other leg. And then eventually it would stop, but then it would start right back up again. I could not move my left leg or my toes in that leg. It was awful. I was on so much pain medicine, but that didn't even *touch* [the pain].

The only way to determine the cause of the spasms was to conduct more MRI's (Magnetic Resonance Images) and more ultrasounds, etc. Trust me, unless you've experienced nerve damage pain, you can't even begin to understand what it must have been like to endure that while undergoing the long and tedious tasks of scan after scan.

Speaking from experience, I would take one hundred needles in the eyeball if I thought it would give me relief. That's pain. And that's what Bonny was feeling when the Lord finally reached down and touched her.

> **B:** There came a point when, mercifully, God let me pass out. During that time, I was ready to go. I didn't think I was going to survive. I was at perfect peace. I have never been at that point in my life. And I just rejoiced! In fact, I'll never forget that when I was at home in my bed [in pain] I was just praising the Lord. I knew that something good was about to happen because he always works it out for our good. We just have to be willing vessels.

That's how faith in the truth works: this incredible survivor credits her harrowing physical experiences with enriching her faith and giving her a closer walk with the Jesus. Despite her suffering, Bonny's countenance radiated Christ's love and the "peace that surpasses understanding" (Philippians 4:7).

> **B:** After my hysterectomy, my boss, Sharon, came to me and said, "Bonny, you've always been a good person, but you're just totally different now. I want that faith and that joy that you have."
>
> And you know I don't even have to force it. It is so real to me. He is as real to me as you are sitting here! (Joyful laugh)
>
> And it saddens me that more Christians don't have that relationship because they don't know what they're missing.
>
> Bad things can't touch us. And here I am back at Romans 8:28 again. Bad things can happen, but He can use those situations to draw us closer. Whatever it takes to bring me closer to Him, because he's not going to give me more than I can handle, because it's in his Word (James 4:8). He's not going to leave me nor forsake me. All the promises of God are "Yea and amen."

Mission: Possible

God *was* going to use this bundle of faith and joy. In June of 2004, while driving to work, Bonny received her mission assignment. Can't you just hear the well-known line from the film and television series, *Mission Impossible:* "Your mission, if you choose to accept it..." The

MI theme plays in my head as I digress, but here's the point: God can speak an assignment to us, but ultimately it's up to us to make the choice to accept it or not. We have to choose to live in obedience to Him.

On that morning, that "still, small voice" (1 Kings 19:11) spoke to Bonny. She was going to start a prayer group...whether she liked it or not.

> **B:** I had a prayer request attached to the dashboard as I always do. And all of a sudden, it wasn't an audible voice but, God spoke to me and said, "I want you to start a prayer group." And I said, "God, I don't want to start a prayer group." I can pray by myself, but I can't pray out loud in front of people." And He said, "I want you to start a prayer group."
>
> Have you ever noticed that in the Bible? God just repeats himself. He doesn't argue with people, He just keeps repeating himself. So I told him for the next two blocks all the reasons why I couldn't start a prayer group. And He said, "Start a prayer group."
>
> So, I asked Him, "Well, what are we going to call the prayer group?" And he came back with "Pots & Pans." And I asked Him what "Pots & Pans" stood for. He said: "**P**rayers of the **S**aints, **P**artnered **A**nd i**N** **S**ync."
>
> And I thought that was so cool.

Bonny immediately set to work, e-mailing her Christian girlfriends who she knew were strong in their walk with the Lord. Starting off in June of 2004 with an original membership of twelve dedicated prayer warriors, Pots & Pans has grown to include a total of 200 members today.

> **B:** We have seen miracle after miracle after miracle happen. We have seen so many answered prayers. It's just so encouraging. I know it blesses my heart, and I feel so honored that the Lord has asked me to do this. And I have grown so much through this.

Shaving Off the Rough Spots

Not long after, Bonny's prayer life hit a bump in the road. Her intercessory anointing was loosing steam. The prayers weren't getting through as they had previously. It wasn't long before the Lord would reveal his next assignment.

As mentioned earlier, Bonny and her mother had been estranged for a number of years. She had been deeply scarred in that relationship and wasn't exactly eager to return for more. But the Lord kept dealing with her about her relationship with her mother.

> **B:** The Lord started reminding me. He said, "Honor your mother." And I said, "I have. I've forgiven her. I don't have any grudge against her. I just don't want to be around her."

While sitting at her desk at work one day, Bonny broke down sobbing and couldn't stop. She felt like Jacob, physically wrestling with the Angel (Genesis 32:24–29). Finally, she was totally exhausted. She sent out some e-mail prayer requests to her pastors and several others, asking them to pray for her regarding her relationship with her mother.

> **B:** I knew I had to do this to get past this hump in my prayer life. But the deep core in this issue was my fear of rejection. And God said, "*I'll never reject you.*" All of a sudden, a little light bulb went off in my head: I don't have to worry about being rejected by anybody because *He is never going to reject me. Praise God!*
>
> The minute I gave in, I received perfect peace. No more tears, just inexplicable joy.
>
> On the way home, I called mom. And the woman, who can never remember phone numbers, remembered her mother's phone number after four years.

The road to reconciliation was being forged. Not long after their phone conversation, Bonny went to visit her mother.

> **B:** You want to talk about a toxic cleansing! It was beautiful. And now we talk about every week or every other week. We see each other about once a month, or however often I can see her due to my

back pain. But it was so nice. I never realized how much I missed her voice.

So the opened heaven prayer channels were back on, but the main thing that I got out of that experience was that I *knew* that I was *being obedient to God.* It was *such* a great feeling. And my prayer life just took off.

Truth Quells Another Storm

All of this prepared Bonny for the difficult season ahead involving her back injury. The spiritual breakthroughs and growth she experienced would give her the strength to *triumph* over yet another challenging period in her life. She grew closer to the Lord than ever before, engaging in an enriching fellowship with Him that she continues to enjoy today.

God works in amazing ways, especially as our prayer lives develop and we draw closer to Him. There are no sweeter sounds to God's ear than when we praise Him during our storms. There are countless scriptures in the Bible testifying to this. In particular, the Psalmists *chose* to praise the Lord despite their changing and overwhelming circumstances. We can *choose* to apply the truth to our tragedy through praise and worship, even in our darkest hours.

Psalm 145, also known as "David's Psalm of Praise" (KJV), illustrates the power of calling on the Lord in times of trouble with *truth-based praise:*

> The Lord is righteous in all His ways and holy in all His works. The Lord is nigh unto all them that call upon Him, to all that call upon Him in truth. He will fulfill the desire of them that fear Him: He also will hear their cry, and save them. The Lord preserveth all them that love Him: but all the wicked will he destroy. My mouth shall speak the praise of the Lord: and let all flesh bless His holy name for ever and ever. (17–21)

Psalm 34 is particularly poignant in its expression, beginning with, "I will bless the Lord at all times: His praise shall continually be in my mouth" *(See end of chapter for additional key scriptures regarding praise)*. Bonny personifies this principle. The Lord will bless us and protect us in our times of trouble, but we have to do our part as well. Prayer, praise and worship are all crucial to our relationship with the Father. And true to His character and promises, the Lord continues to reward His faithful servants.

> **B:** I *love* my prayer time with Him. I have a prayer closet at home. And the people He has brought into my path during all of this have been unreal. Take my friend, Allison, for example. Here's how God works: I'm at the hospital and they're about to discharge me. It was on a Monday, the day after that terrible back and leg pain hit me, and thought I was going to die. I asked Luke to please call Miss Joan, a prayer warrior from church, to come pray for me. And she came. I just remember waking up to see her standing by my bed, holding her bible. And I just started crying.
>
> I remember a bunch of people standing around my bed, and I remember her praying for me. I started getting better after that. I was able to go home just a few days later. The muscle spasms and nerve pain had disappeared. All I had left to recover from was the surgery.

Not only would the prayers of a righteous "woman" availeth much (variation on James 5:16, KJV), she would also represent the link between Bonny and her much needed help mate and future friend, Allison.

After leaving the hospital, Miss Joan attended a Christmas party. It was there that she had a conversation with a mutual friend, Teresa. And again, God, the Master Planner, had set the wheels in motion, providing everything that Bonny would need.

> **B:** Teresa almost didn't go that night, but something kept telling her that she needed to go. She told Miss Joan that Allison had just been laid off, and that if she knew of anybody who needed help doing *anything* to please let Allison know.
>
> That was on Monday night. On Wednesday night, I called up Miss Joan and said, "They're going to discharge me either today or tomorrow, and I'm going to need someone to stay with me at the

house during the day while Luke's at work." And she said, "As a matter of fact, I do."

Enter Allison, stage left: a single mom with two children, who had just lost her job. In addition, Allison was dealing with the recent loss of her mother. In God's perfect wisdom and timing, he brought these two women of faith together at a time when each desperately needed what the other had to offer—a coincidence? I think not. I can't say this enough: God is so good and he's always on time... especially when we're walking in obedience, Amen!

> **B:** Allison started to come to stay with me and we became fast friends. We realized we had a lot of things in common. Through all of this, her ministering to me has just blessed my heart. And I've been able to offer her words of encouragement along the way.
>
> Then when it was time for me to go back to work (the doctor didn't want me to, but I wanted to try), I hadn't been released to drive.

Where others might have seen an obstacle, Bonny saw an opportunity. She contacted Sharon and presented a solution that would benefit everyone concerned.

> **B:** I said to Sharon, "I can't drive, and you're paying a temp 'x' amount of dollars to sit at the front desk and answer phones. You could hire my friend, Allison, who needs a job. She could drive me to work on the days that I can come, as long as she could come to the office the rest of the time.
>
> And Sharon agreed to it, God bless her. And that's the only reason that I'm able to be here now. And Allison turned out to be a good fit. Sharon has told me that she likes Allison, that she's smart, she's bright, she's great, she is such a 'find'. So, it's been good for Allison!
>
> And here's another thing. There are so many strong Christians in [that office] right now. And one day I was walking across the bridge to the car...and I'm surprised you didn't hear me shout! God showed me how he had strong Christians in every corner of that floor. I

believe that He has planted us here to be a light to [our Jewish colleagues]. We're *exactly* where we're supposed to be.

Bonny explains how and why she has always felt a special calling on her life to witness to God's chosen people:

> **B:** All of my life, the Lord has put people in my life to teach me about the Jewish people and the Jewish customs. Our friends, the Shipley's [the same family who took Bonny under their wing when she was a child], were charter members of "Jewish Believers and Friends" in the early '70's in the Atlanta area.
>
> So all my life, the Lord has been equipping me to witness to Jewish people about the Messiah. He has really given Luke and me a love for the Jewish people. And because of that, whenever Jewish friends or co-workers ask me questions, I'm equipped to answer them.

Where Are They Now?

Today, Bonny and Luke live just south of Atlanta, Georgia. She recently returned to work full-time at a global public relations firm in Atlanta and continues to pray a hedge of protection around her co-workers. Bonny and Luke are active members in their church.

Pots & Pans, the powerful intercessory prayer chain, has grown to include over 200 members.

In addition, this tireless servant has recently founded "The House of Ruth," a place of intercessory prayer, praise and worship, Bible study, and services that marry the Jew and the Gentile in Messianic Christian Study. Their website describes their mission as follows:

> "The House of Ruth" is made up of Christians who are hungry for a move of God, like the people in the New Testament church enjoyed, before it became bound up in the traditions of man.
>
> God has installed in each of our hearts a strong love for Israel and her people. Jew and Gentile in fellowship together like Naomi and

Ruth, worshipping together like the one new man Paul speaks of in his epistle to the church in Ephesus. [11]

And Luke has also answered God's calling on his life. Sadly enough, methamphetamine use is on the rise in the South Georgia. But again, Romans 8:28 pops up: God is using Luke's experience and background. He is currently counseling people who are struggling with addiction to meth. He is also mentoring young boys who don't have a father figure, or who are dealing with severe rejection.

B: I am just so thankful for every day. Luke and I have been through so much. We have an appreciation for each other we've never felt before.

But sometimes I think I don't "get it" because I don't worry enough, that I'm not anxious enough; because I'm anxious for nothing (Matthew 6:31). However, I was anxious for a time as to how long it is taking to recuperate from back surgery. Different people told me stories about how they knew someone who was up and around in no time after their back surgery. I was a little anxious then, wondering what was wrong with *me*. *They* made me anxious (laughing). But now that I've gotten into the spirit that *God is in control,* I am no longer anxious about that either.

Because we have free will, we can choose; but *God's plan is going to happen* (Phil: 4:6–7, 19**).** What I've gone through has made me the person I am today. So I may as well sit back and let Him drive the train!

As for Bonny's parents, they divorced in 1984 after thirty years of marriage. Her father could no longer live with effects of alcoholism. He was saved (Praise God!) and attends Bible Study every Tuesday. Praise God again: Bonny's mother has been sober for eighteen years, and mother and daughter continue to work at their relationship.

Bonny's story is rife with examples of what happens when we wait on the Lord and trust in Him. We can count on Him to weave the circumstances together and come up with the solution: providing the right people and/or resources at just the right time. There are no coincidences. He is our awesome provider and we can trust Him to do that...especially during our seasons of tragedy.

> **B:** I can see God's hand in everything. Everything is so much sweeter and brighter. I thank God every day for the ability to get up out of bed on my own, because there was a time when I couldn't do that. I just can't wait to see what he's going to do with my day! Especially since the back injury, my spiritual eyes have been opened. Now I can see Him at work in the *present tense* instead of "in hindsight." Today, I live with the anticipation of "what does God have planned for me next?"
>
> Like the blind man that Jesus healed by putting mud on his eyes, I've been touched once and I eagerly await—yea expect—the second touch that will bring me complete healing. But even if that day never comes (though I have faith that it will), I will align myself with what the Apostle Paul shared with us in 2 Corinthians 12:8–10 (NIV):
>
>> Concerning this thing I pleaded with the Lord...that it might depart from me. And He said to me, "My Grace is sufficient for you, for My strength is made perfect in weakness.' Therefore most gladly I will rather boast in my infirmities, that the power of Christ may rest upon me. Therefore I take pleasure in infirmities, in reproaches, in needs, in persecutions, in distresses, for Christ's sake. For when I am weak, then I am strong."

During the course of our interview, I officially became member number 201 of Pots & Pans. Bonny's enthusiasm is infectious. You just can't help wanting to become part of what she is pursuing...a closer walk with the Lord every day of her life.

Though partially disabled, she is *walking evidence* that through His truth, we can emerge from our tragedies, triumphant and strong, singing His praises in the good times and the bad. We can grow to become an irresistible example of what it means to know Christ: to have Him as Lord in our lives; to know what it means to have that uncompromising 3T Vision.

* Special Note:

If you are interested in becoming a member of the *Pots & Pans* intercessory prayer group, you may contact Bonny at potspans@windstream.net.

To learn more about *The House of Ruth*, click on www.houseofruth-thomaston.org.

> Entreat me not to leave thee, or to return from the following after thee: for wither thou go; and where thou lodgest, I will lodge: thy people shall be my people, and thy God my God.
>
> Ruth 1:16 (KJV)

Additional Scriptures

Theme: praising the Lord during the storms
Psalms 34:17–19, 56, 57, 59:16–17, 69:30–36, 96, 107, 118, 136, 144:3–4, 145:14, 147–150

Acts
16: 22–26

Reflections

Chapter 6

Mary's Story
Blessed Be the Name of Mary
(The Power of the Holy Spirit and a Praying Mother)

I love all my kids, but there was something unusual about Kyle. I just knew I wasn't going to get to keep him very long.

I believe a lot of souls were saved because of his death...When I die, I want to be at Jesus' feet. I just want to wrap my arms around his legs and hug him. I have so much to be grateful for.

Miss Mary

And the Lord said unto Moses, Is the Lord's hand waxed short? Thou shalt see now whether my word shall come to pass unto thee or not. (Numbers 11:23, KJV)

The Interview

The first time Miss Mary and I got together to tape her story, we ended up sharing a classic Southern country meal of pork chops, butter beans, and macaroni and cheese. Before I knew it, a few hours filled with fellowship and laughter had passed, and we hadn't even turned the tape recorder on. I found myself lost, once again, in her autobiographical stories; always rich in Southern history, folk-lore, and personalities you will never forget. She has that rare talent of combining a tragic tale with comedic relief. One moment you're horrified, the next you're laughing until your sides split.

On my second attempt at our interview, Miss Mary greeted me with her characteristic bear hug and a freshly baked chocolate cake. Light-heartedly, I reminded my sweet friend that as much as I love her *and* her cooking, we needed to stay focused on the telling of her poignant testimony that needed to be told. So we made ourselves comfortable in her modest, one-bedroom apartment, decorated primarily with family photos and Christian ornaments. Over the next few hours, the sixty-five-year-old widow would share her story of triumph over tragedy.

The Long Arm of the Lord

When John and Mary brought their newborn baby home from the hospital in April of 1966, they immediately knew there was something wrong. Little Kyle cried constantly. After four sleepless nights, they took him back to the Atlanta area hospital. The emergency room doctor told them their baby had an infection. He prescribed an antibiotic and sent the family home.

Not long after, Kyle began gasping for breath. Leaving John at home to watch over their three other children, Mary rushed the baby back to the hospital. This time, they admitted him. Her family doctor told her Kyle should never have been sent home. Not only did their precious baby boy have a hole in his heart, one of his lungs had collapsed!

Mary sent for her husband. After receiving additional test results, the doctor gave the couple the worst news a parent could hear. Kyle wasn't expected to live until morning. They were devastated.

> **M:** This was just too much for me. I felt like jumping out of the window. But I didn't. As terrified as I was, I knew there was a God. I had been raised in the Church, but had drifted away in recent years.
>
> In their moment of utter despair however, Mary and John chose to appeal to God and rely on the promises of His word. Instinctively, they knew that even though they had put Him on the back burner, He would be there for them in their hour of need as promised in

> Joshua 1:5 (KJV) "...so I will be with thee: I will not fail thee, nor forsake thee."

The doctors had brought their dismal report. The couple could have relied on their own understanding, the reports of the natural world, or they could turn their *vision* back to God's *truth*. It was at this moment that Mary recalled the scripture (Numbers 11:23, NIV) wherein God reminded Moses of his awesome power and reach. This scripture would become the centerpiece of Mary's prayer life for Kyle.

> The Lord answered Moses, "Is the Lord's arm too short? You will now see whether or not what I say will come true for you."

So, in that sterile, cold hospital room, the young parents dropped to their knees and prayed. Through their tears they begged the Lord to reach out and touch their little boy who lay gasping for his next breath. Overcome with conviction that the Lord could, and would, heal their baby boy despite the prognosis, Mary and John took their prayer a step further:

> **M:** We promised the Lord that if he let our child live we would dedicate the rest of our lives to Him.

Wasting no time, Mary sought out additional prayer support. She called her aunt, a godly woman, who put Kyle on a prayer chain. Her next call was to her brother, Robert, a preacher.

True to His word, God began to work as He always does when we turn to Him. Because, in fact, there was another mother on that floor, a staunch Believer, whose child was also in peril. The little boy had been hit by a taxi. The doctors claimed he was paralyzed and would never walk again. As mothers in such situations do, the two bonded, sharing their feelings and faith.

The mother of the paralyzed boy (Mary cannot recall her name) refused to give up. The Oral Roberts Crusade was in town, in Atlanta, that night and she was going to take her son's t-shirt with her to the revival. She graciously offered to take one of Kyle's too. Demonstrating her faith once again, Mary provided the woman with one of Kyle's shirts. Relying on the *truth*, one woman, with faith in her heart and two small t-shirts in hand, saw Oral Roberts and made her requests known to God:

> Do not be anxious about anything, but in everything, by prayer and petition, with thanksgiving, present your requests to God. And the peace of God, which transcends all understanding, will guard your hearts and minds in Christ Jesus.
>
> Philippians 4:6–7, KJV

Not three days later, the doctors announced that both boys had been "cured by a higher power." And again, as in my own story, the physicians took no credit for their tiny patients' recovery.

> **M:** It was a miracle! They could no longer find the whole in Kyle's heart, and his lung was normal! And the other little boy was moving his legs!

Both families were ecstatic to say the least. All of the prayers emanating from a tiny hospital room, a humble country church, and a throng of crusaders had been answered. The mighty arm of God had indeed reached down and touched the two children.

God Begins a Good Work (Jeremiah 29:11)

Finally, Mary and John were able to bring Kyle home. And as often happens, Mary admits, once their worries had been lifted, she and John allowed their promise to God slide for a short time. But the fear of God, the reverence for him, had stayed with Mary. She felt led to attend her family's church in her home town, just north of Atlanta.

At first, John would just drop Mary and Kyle off at the church to attend services. Suffering from a rheumatic heart condition, Mary was too weak to take all of the children. But after a season of relentless praying on her part, her husband finally took up the cross as well. The family moved back to their home town and joined the church.

M: We had the children dedicated. And I have never quit going to church since that day.

Her prayers answered, Mary watched her husband grow closer and closer to the Lord. Always having been a very charismatic man, John became a Sunday school teacher, played different instruments and sang in the music ministry. He finally began to preach. And he began to fast. She began to notice that the lunches she prepared for him would still be in his lunchbox when he returned home from work every day.

In addition, Mary took on the position of Assistant Director of Children's Sunday school, directing all of the programs and the choir. The family had made the decision to serve the Lord and immerse their children in a life dedicated to Jesus. They seemed to personify the scripture, "as for me and my house, we shall serve the Lord." (Joshua 24:15).

All five children (Julie, Michael, Sheila, Kyle and Cindy) were eventually saved, praise God. And they were all talented in their own way. But 12-year-old Kyle and 14-year-old Julie were especially anointed in their singing ministry. Kyle also played the drums, while his sister played the guitar.

M: Whenever they performed they were truly inspirational. The Pentecostal congregation would actually run up and down the aisles. We didn't realize it at the time, but in working for the Lord, our family was planting seeds in generations of children to come.

Tragedy Strikes

But this period of serving the Lord was not to last forever. The enticements of the World were beginning to encroach on her husband and her teenage children. Marital problems plagued Mary and John. And by the time they had gotten to middle school, Kyle and Julie had begun to lose interest in church services, but still attended Sunday school and Vacation Bible School. Once in high school, they had stopped going to church all together.

M: As hard as I tried, I could not get them to go. It broke my heart, but I continued to pray for them.

Then one month after graduation, Kyle announced that he was going to marry his girlfriend, Lisa. He was eighteen and she was just sixteen-years-old. Lisa was pregnant, and their baby girl, Ashley, was born in August, just two months later. I begged Kyle not to get married at such a young age, but he wouldn't listen. Looking back now, I believe he knew that his time on earth would be brief. He wanted to experience having a wife and a child. Kyle would often say things like, "My time's running out, Mama. I've got to get things done quickly."

Despite Kyle's intense love for Lisa, the relationship was strained from the beginning. In fact, before Ashley was two, it was clear her parents were going their separate ways.

While Lisa and Kyle worked, Mary and John, and Lisa's parents, Jimmy and Paula Jones cared for Ashley. On that fateful night, however, the Jones were going to a dinner party, so Mary and John agreed to pick their granddaughter up from their home. Mary remembers seeing Kyle's truck in the yard. When she asked Jimmy where Kyle was, he informed her that Kyle had left with a boy named Curtis.

M: It was like a dagger went through my heart when I heard that. I can't even explain the feeling that came over me. I believe the Holy Ghost was telling me something was wrong. I started to pray. Curtis had a really bad reputation of being a bully. Kyle knew I didn't want him any where near that boy.

On their way home, they picked up Mary's oldest daughter, Julie, who was also experiencing marital problems.

Mary remembers it was a very hot summer evening. A heavy, ominous feeling lingered in the air. Trying to ignore it, she stayed busy by giving her granddaughter a bath. Then, as she was hanging up some clothes in front of a shelf that Kyle had bought for her, she felt an unmistakable tap on the top of her head.

M: That tap went through my entire body. And I just knew it was the Holy Ghost. And He said to me, "Sadness will come over this house and many tears shall be shed." Then the Holy Ghost led me down the hallway. It had me kneel down beside the coffee table and it told me how to pray. I said, "Lord, I don't know who this is for, but you do. Whatever their need is Lord, you know what it is."

Relying once again on Numbers 11:23, Mary prayed: *"Reach down and help them Lord."*

Mary and John began to cry. Then John reached over and touched his wife's hand, demonstrating a tenderness that was uncharacteristic of him. But this would be anything but an ordinary night.

> *M:* (her voice brimming with emotion):
> I just wanted to get out and run and keep running. I told John and Julie about the message I had received and we all began to cry together.
>
> When the Holy Ghost warns you about something like that, you need to listen. But at the time, I thought that whatever was going to happen would be farther off (in the future). I had no idea it was going to happen right then.

Mary tried several times to get undressed to take a shower, but felt as though the Holy Ghost would not allow it. When her granddaughter fell asleep, she decided to lie down as well. Around midnight, the telephone rang.

> **M:** That was the worst ring I had ever heard. And then I heard Julie screaming in the other room. I ran to my daughter.

The ominous feeling and anointed message had been confirmed. It was Lisa who had called to tell them that Kyle had been killed in a car wreck.

> **M:** I just started screaming. I ran back to the bed, knelt down, and began to pray. But the Holy Ghost told me to get up, get dressed and get to the hospital as fast as possible.
>
> We raced to the E.R. I remember pulling into the parking lot as if it were yesterday.

John didn't even stop to turn off the engine before we ran in. And it was true. The doctors and nurses were working on Kyle in the back room. The entire right side of his face had collapsed. It took them four hours to reconstruct his face. We later learned that the truck had apparently flipped over several times and Kyle's head had been caught between the tire and the rim. The police later told us that the three other passengers received only minor cuts and bruises.

The scene at the hospital was chaotic. Kyle's in-laws were very distraught, having loved him as a son.

Out of her mind with grief, Mary roamed the hospital corridors sobbing, just as she had done twenty-one years before. But this time, no amount of praying, no promises to God would bring her son back. Angry, hurt, feeling betrayed, she demanded of God, *"Why didn't you let me know this was going to happen?"*

M: But then I realized that the Holy Spirit *had* tried to tell me that something was wrong. Just a week before the accident, I had been praying for my daughter, Sheila, when the Lord interrupted me. He told me to pray for Kyle. I felt so sad when the Lord said this. I remember praying, "Lord, if I knew that Kyle was safe with you, I wouldn't have to worry." The Lord knew Kyle was going through something then, but I didn't know it. Then the Lord told me that Kyle had died for a specific reason.

Although Mary didn't understand what that meant at the time, the Holy Spirit would later whisper a revelation to John during Kyle's funeral.

In the meantime, Mary and John collected themselves enough to take Lisa and Ashley home from the hospital.

M: I remember crying uncontrollably as I walked up the walkway that Kyle had built. Our home was filled that night with friends and family when we returned from the hospital. We stayed up all night. Nobody could have slept.

After everyone had left, Sheila and I were lying on the couches in the living room. John came in to the room. He was crying, and he asked me, "Mary, do you know where Kyle is?"

And once again, the Holy Ghost came over me. And I said, "He is with Jesus. He is with Jesus." Then the Holy Ghost washed over both me and my daughter. Sheila confirmed the message when she announced, *"He is with the Lord! He is with the Lord!"*

The next day, Mary, John, Sheila and Lisa shopped for the clothes that Kyle would be buried in. True to his down-to-earth nature, Kyle had always insisted that, when his time came, he wanted to be buried in blue jeans and a shirt. On the way into the department store, Mary recalls a cluster of butterflies following them in, and then landing on them as they left.

> **M:** Then again at the funeral, yet another flock of butterflies flew about during the ceremony. It was just too much of a coincidence. Since butterflies are symbolic of life, I felt that God may have been trying to tell me that Kyle had found everlasting life.
>
> During the funeral, I spoke in tongues constantly while John sat beside me, praying.
>
> And then John received a message from the Holy Ghost: "I saw him in trouble, so I reached down and got him."

Again, that familiar scripture rang true for Mary: nothing was beyond God's reach. Confirmation of this message came just moments later when one of Kyle's elementary school teachers approached them. Telling them how sweet he had been as a little boy, she added that the Lord had told her Kyle was indeed "with the one true God."

The Emotional Fall-Out

> **M:** After the funeral, I began to experience insomnia and panic attacks. I couldn't breathe. My best friend, Audrey, prayed with me through those spells. I leaned on her literally and spiritually.

Two memories in particular haunted the grieving mother, plunging her further into an already deep depression. Sometimes it's the simple moments, the simple memories that trouble us as we grieve. Mary had always given Kyle cologne for Christmas, but the year before his death, she had decided to buy him a sweater instead.

> **M:** (Her voice cracks as tears well up in her eyes once again)
>
> I remember he hugged me and asked, "Mama, I love my sweater, but why didn't you buy me some cologne?" And all I could think was, *"Why didn't I buy him some cologne?"*

In another instance, about a week before his death, Kyle had come to pick Ashley up from his mother's house one night after work. Mary had been looking after the baby all day and had just finished cooking dinner for the family. Kyle asked his mother to make him something special for dinner. Tired and irritable, Mary had asked Kyle to eat what she had already prepared.

> **M:** I wish I had cooked him that meal, but I was just so tired. When Kyle left that night, he turned and kissed me goodbye before leaving. I remember standing still in the same spot until he returned a few seconds later, as if I *knew* he was coming right back.
>
> He came back in and he hugged me so tightly. And I hugged him back. And he said, "Mama, I really do love you." He was telling me goodbye. It was the last time I saw him before he died. I'll never forget it.

As if this one tragedy wasn't enough, Kyle's death would be just one of three deaths that Mary and her family would endure that year.

> **M:** I lost my mother in January of 1987, Kyle was killed that summer, and my father passed away that fall. It got to the point that it hurt so badly that I wanted to die. I think losing a child is even harder to take than losing a parent or a spouse.

It was the day before Thanksgiving that Mary's mental state was pushed to the breaking point. .

> **M:** I was so angry with God. I asked Him, "Why did you have to take my child and no one else's child was even hurt?"

She went to church that night with her family despite her despair. But she couldn't stay still. A constant wave washed over her that she couldn't escape. The pastor prayed over her, but to no avail. He urged John to take Mary to the hospital.

Mary was admitted to the hospital that night. Because it wasn't possible for her to be seen by a psychiatrist until the next day, it was decided that she be put in "lock-up" to prevent her from hurting herself.

Grieving to a point that she could no longer cope, Mary ended up spending a few weeks in the psychiatric wing. Once again, the Lord came through for her in her hour of need. He surrounded the fragile woman with friends and doctors that would help see her through this part of the journey. As described in Isaiah 43:20–21 (NIV), our faithful Father would provide Mary with:

> "…water in the desert and streams in the wasteland, to give drink to my people, my chosen, the people I formed for myself that they may proclaim my praise."

Mary's doctor finally convinced her to take medications that would enable her to sleep and eat.

> **M:** I hadn't slept more than a few hours a night in five or six months. I couldn't eat. I couldn't even swallow water. I was constantly sick to my stomach. Up until that point I feared the persecution of my church. They didn't believe in taking any medication that was, what they considered to be, "mind altering."

The Road to Recovery

With proper rest and nutrition, Mary began to recover. And as any true Believer knows, there are no coincidences. It turned out that a good friend of Mary's was working as a nurse at the facility. And one of her neighbors was also receiving treatment at the same time.

> **M:** I just know that God worked that out for me. Having people up there that I was familiar with helped me a lot.

Additional catharsis would follow when the doctors introduced Mary to a young girl who had lost her boyfriend in a car accident. The two women immediately bonded. Again, there are no coincidences. The good Lord connected these two women, one lost, one found, and both in need of healing. Mary took the lead, making herself available to the Lord. She would put aside her own hurt for a moment to share the good news with a lost soul. Mary asked the young girl if she could pray for her.

> **M:** I told her not be frightened if I started speaking in tongues (with a light laugh).

Finding comfort in each other, they began to pray together regularly. During one of their worship sessions, Mary felt led by the Holy Ghost to witness to the patients in wheelchairs.

> **M:** I went out and talked to every one of them. I told them they didn't have to be there–that there was a Jesus they could call on.

The following morning, Mary was released from lock-up. She was now able to participate in activities that could further facilitate her recovery. It was during this time that Mary made the conscious and miraculous decision to remain an open vessel for Jesus. She and another young man began daily devotional meetings.

> **M:** The Lord was going to use me. I believe a lot of souls were saved because of Kyle's death.
>
> And I do remember the beautiful sunrises coming up. There were only a few of us sitting out on our little balcony every morning, enjoying that devotional. It was wonderful.

This woman, who could have become a self-indulgent, bitter, pitiful psychiatric vegetable, decided instead to obey God and keep the vision for salvation that he has for all of us. Instead of wallowing in self-pity, Mary found strength in the Lord and resumed her role as a witness to His truth, grace and mercy. He had provided her with the renewing water in the wasteland, and she was proclaiming His praises.

Relying on Him, and believing in His promises, a prayerful and witnessing mother managed to turn her son's tragic death into blessings for others.

Imagine it! While in the midst of her own private tempest, enduring one of the deepest forms of pain there is, locked up in a psychiatric ward, this woman chose to continue to testify that *truth triumphs over tragedy!* Hallelujah! By relying on the word and the Holy Spirit, she turned her suffering into testimony to others.

As Pastor Joel Osteen explains, *In Your Best Life Now:* when in need, God will bless us if we sow a seed:

> When you meet other people's needs, God has promised that He will make sure your needs are supplied. If you want to see healing and restoration come to your life, go out and help somebody else get well. The Bible says, "In times of difficulty, trust in the Lord and do good"
>
> Psalm 37:1–3 NIV. [12] (251)

And that's exactly what Mary had done. What a testimony to the resilience of the human spirit and faithfulness of God when we reach out to Him!

Although she didn't feel quite ready, Mary was released from the hospital just before Christmas.

> **M:** I felt as though my family needed me. That Christmas was so difficult for me. At times I felt numb and fought off panic attack after panic attack. I couldn't have made it through that holiday season without the Holy Ghost.

God's Grace and Mercy–The Revelation

After the holidays, Mary felt strong enough to return to teaching Children's Sunday school. And as if to reward her for her continued obedience, the Lord had a special gift in store for her—the precious peace that she so desperately longed for.

It happened one morning while she stood over the kitchen sink washing dishes. Melting into tears, Mary begged God to confirm what she had always felt in her heart: that Kyle was in heaven.

M: I just wanted to know where he was and how he was feeling.

As she prayed and appealed to God, her ebbing panic attack ceased, replaced by that inexplicable peace. Again, Mary obeyed the Lord. She felt as though he was leading her over to the kitchen table where she always kept a pen and notebook to record ideas for Sunday school.

The following poem flowed from pen to paper:

Don't worry about me,
I'm where I should be.
I'm at home with my Father above,
Where I'll always be loved.
Cry for the ones behind,
That Satan has bound.
Fast for the souls to be saved,
Before it's too late.
Soon I'll come out of my grave.
Don't cry anymore,
Smile and rejoice.
For we'll be together again,
When my Father descends.
So tell everyone you meet,
For me don't weep.
For I'm in paradise,
Where Jesus Christ is my light.

Bursting with joy and relief beyond words, Mary showed the poem to John. Together, they shed tears of joy. After sharing the poem with the rest of the family, they decided to have it engraved on Kyle's headstone.

The imparting of this poem proved to be a turning point for the hurting mother.

M: You never truly get over that pain, but at the moment that God gave me that poem I was able to get on with my life.

The Bible says that God will not abandon the grieving mother. His love and comfort for her is illustrated in Jeremiah 31: 13–17 (NIV). But He especially rewards the mother who turns from constant weeping and grieving; who turns her grief into positive work for the Lord.

"…I will turn their mourning into gladness; I will give them comfort and joy instead of sorrow.

…This is what the Lord says: "A voice is heard in Ramah, mourning and great weeping, Rachel weeping for her children and refusing to be comforted, because her children are no more.

…Restrain your voice from weeping and your eyes from tears, for your work will be rewarded," declares the Lord.

"They will return from the land of the enemy. So there is hope for your future," declares the Lord.

"Your children will return to their own land."

Mary had turned her grief into testimony for others and the Lord had freed her with the poem; letting her know that even though her son had strayed from the church in recent years, he was, indeed, in heaven.

M: Then one night, the Lord spoke to me again as I rocked on my porch swing. He said, "Blessed be the name of Mary" (Luke 1:48). At that moment I so identified with both Mary and God. They too felt the pain of losing a son, but their son had to take on all the pain of the world, every pain that we had ever felt! I also took that message to mean that I had been faithful in praying for my children and grandchildren, but that I needed to continue to pray for them. When I die, I want to be at Jesus' feet. I just want to wrap my arms around his legs and hug him. I have so much to be grateful for.

Mary credits the Holy Ghost for bringing her through her loss and then her stay in the hospital. But equally true is that she *chose* to keep her eyes on the Lord throughout her ordeal. Even though her mental state was clouded at times because of the intense pain she was feeling, her *spiritual vision* remained clear.

Again, holding on to God's promise that nothing was beyond his grasp, and the fact that he would "never leave her nor forsake her," she continued to pray herself through. And when she didn't have the strength to pray herself through, she relied on the prayer warriors around her to appeal to the Lord for herself and her family.

So many of us forget to reach out to others for prayer; fearing that we'll appear to be weak or unable to pray ourselves through. But God's word reminds us that where two or more are gathered, He is in our midst (Matthew 18:20). Mary recognized that truth, and allowed her Christian friends to prayerfully intercede for her as she continued to recover.

She may have been discouraged and angry at times, as any mother would, but she *never turned away from the truth.* Time and time again, Mary turned toward the face of Jesus. She "prayed without ceasing" (1 Thessalonians 5:17) and encouraged others to do the same. In the end, our loving God poured out His triumph over her tragedy.

Today

Still a resident of North Georgia, Mary enjoys a close relationship with her four remaining children, 13 grandchildren and one great-grandson. She visits with them often. John passed away in January of 2004. Having been married to him for 45 years, Mary still misses him very much, but stays busy with family, friends and church activities.

The outgoing, sweet soul, that she is, Mary regularly takes food to neighbors, prays for them, and has hosted prayer meetings in her living room. She continues to submerge herself in the Word: the *truth* that *has* and *will* continue to see her through life's tragedies and on to triumph.

Additional Scripture

*Theme: Grief (*KJV, LASB*)*
Freedom to grieve—Genesis 50:1–11
Don't be ashamed to grieve—2 Samuel 1:11–12
Job 1:20–22
Moving from grief to action—Nehemiah 1:4(2)
Can't take away life's real purpose—Job 3:23–26
How Jesus handled grief—Matthew 14:13–14

Meditate on this scripture when feeling mentally, emotionally or spiritually unstable.
2 Timothy 1:7

Reflections

Chapter 7

The Author's 2nd Testimony:
3T Vision Goes Full-Circle

And let us not lose heart and grow weary and faint in acting nobly
and doing right, for in due time and at the appointed season we shall
reap, if we do not loosen and relax our courage and faint.

Galatians 6:9 (Amplified Bible)

Well, dear readers, just when I thought I had shared my one pivotal
testimony for this book, the Lord saw fit to send me another...and
another...and another. In hindsight, I truly believe that the Lord's
plan to bring this book to its perfect completion was to bring my
two testimonies full circle. The first testimony spawned the concept
for the book, and the second would lend credence to the message of
"3T Vision."

I had no idea when I began writing this book, that the final chapter would involve my family once again. Some families can go for
generations without a single tragedy befalling them, and I praise
God for that. Others, like mine, however, seem to personify the saying, "When it rains, it pours."

In His infinite wisdom, the Master Planner took the havoc that
the enemy threw at me during the course of those eighteen months,
and, again, turned it around for my good and His glory (Romans

8:28). Instead of giving up and packing it in, the good Lord arranged for me to live the *vision* up-close-and-personal once again, *as I was completing the book!* He was providing me with a renewed passion for the vision, and at the same time, a deeper meaning to the work.

Even though I was dealing with my father's and stepmother's health crisis; the adjustments involved when my mother-in-law moved in after Hurricane Katrina struck; and my 18-year-old niece moving in; *the job got done: 3T Vision* became a reality.

I once heard it said that one's character is revealed during unexpected circumstances. Because it's not a matter of *if*, but rather *when*, we are going to face trials and temptations. The Book of James is chock full of how Christians *should* behave when facing adversity. When we trust God and ask for strength during difficult times, we can expect a positive outcome. Periods of adversity teach us patience and result in spiritual maturity.

> My brethren, count it all joy when ye fall into divers temptations;
> Knowing this, that the trying of your faith worketh patience. But
> let patience have her perfect work, that ye may be perfect and entire,
> wanting nothing.
>
> James 1:2–4, KJV

As much as I would like to claim that I was a stellar example of unshakeable strength, patience and faith during this time, I humbly admit I had to constantly fight off feelings of frustration, anxiety and depression. The demands that these new trials placed on me, and the energy and time they consumed, constantly challenged my ability to focus on, and write for, God.

In addition, I worried about how all of the changes were affecting my 6-year-old little boy, and whether or not he was getting the attention he needed. For a while, Larry and I became little more than two ships passing in the night. The resulting stress stirred up negative emotions, which threatened my health, my relationships and the completion of *3T Vision.*

There were times that I was so overwhelmed, so exhausted, that I didn't even have the words to pray. Relying on the Holy Spirit to intercede for me, I would lie on the floor in my office and just cry out to Jesus.

And then, supernaturally, the Lord would pick me up, dust me off, and give me the renewed strength and creativity I needed to fulfill the *vision*. The faithful prayer of friends and family (especially my husband) cannot be understated either. This book would not be a reality had I not been covered up in, and lifted up by, prayer during this time.

Everything that was happening made no sense at first (does it ever?). Again, I was reminded of Isaiah 55:8–9, wherein God tells us that "[His] thoughts are not our thoughts, neither are [His] ways our ways...For as the heavens are higher than the earth, so are [His] ways higher than [our] ways and [His] thoughts than [our] thoughts" (KJV).

But I found myself asking, "Why would the Lord give me the concept for this book, open the door to have it published, and then allow the cares of the world to snuff it all out?" Then it hit me: the trials that I first believed to be obstacles to completing the work, in fact, became *enhancers* of the work!

The outcome of it all would hinge on my attitude. And trust me—at times my attitude could be smelled as far away as Alaska. It was made clear from the outset that the Lord was going to test my faith while writing His book. He wanted me to *walk the walk* while I *wrote the talk!*

Not six weeks after signing the contract to write the book, tragedy after tragedy touched my life. It was as if the enemy decided he was going to throw every obstacle he could at me, in an attempt to distract and discourage me from completing the *vision*. Saints, any time we take on a task which is meant to glorify the Lord and touch the hearts of many, we are going to rattle the enemy's cages. If the enemy can't convince us to denounce our faith, he'll throw every curve ball our way to prevent us from fulfilling God's purpose for our lives.

So one of the first things I had to do was to make a faith decision to trust in Him to send me the right women with the right testimonies. And He did: Glory to God!

And because of the constraints on my writing time, I prayed and asked God to anoint my every moment at the keyboard. Not only did He make my writing time productive, He placed the right Christian books, television and radio messages, articles and sermons in my path that would enrich the content of this book (You'll notice several quotations from Pastor Olsteen and Joyce Meyer because I was reading their books while writing the final chapter).

It was as though the Lord had a plan and purpose for every faith message I would receive during this time! Whether I was at home, or in the car, I was constantly searching for paper and pen to copy down the truths that He was sending my way. Many of the messages just helped to bolster my faith during a stressful time. God is so good.

How awesome that we have a dependable Father who we can turn to for strength, peace, wisdom and courage. And of course, the Lord always comes through and we can complete His mission for our lives; spreading the gospel despite the hardships that befall us. Jesus' promise found in John 10:10 can never be stressed enough: "the thief comes only to steal and kill and destroy; I have come that they may have life and life more abundantly" (NIV).

As stressful as it was to have the responsibility of completing God's book while facing several personal crises, I don't know what I would have done without it. Did God know that I would need a diversion during this time? As it turned out, the book actually became a source of much-needed spiritual fuel. Each interview, the writing of each chapter, inspired me and led me from faith to faith. Over and over again, God's grace and mercy, his unfailing power was revealed to me. I thank Him for anointing me to write and testify of His miraculous works during this season of tribulation. In hindsight, as challenging as it was at times to focus on the vision, (on *3T Vision!*) the vision itself became an oasis in the desert, an emotional and psychological shelter in the storm.

I'm going to be painfully honest here. When I first signed the contract for this book, I was elated. I was finally going to take on my life-long dream to write a book. But first and foremost, I was going to realize my dream to work for God, utilizing the talent He has so graciously given me.

But elation soon turned to apprehension: "Who am *I?*" I asked. "Am I mature enough in my walk with Christ to be effective as a messenger for Him?" I doubted myself. And when you do that, you give a foothold to the enemy. That's when the arrows started flying. But those arrows forced me to put on the whole armor of God (Ephesians 6:10–17).

I began to grow as a Christian at high speed seeking a more intimate relationship with Him. I prayed, read Scripture and repented as never before. At times, I literally got down on *my* face to seek *His* face.

So here we are. Not only did the Lord give me the strength, courage and peace I asked for to finish His book, He also gave me several very special gifts: the contents for the final chapter; the maternal maturity I had so longed for; and, most importantly, the spiritual maturity and intimacy with Him that I desired. The following story describes the trials and tragedies that most recently challenged my family and how, through His truth, we triumphed once again.

The Roller-Coaster Ride Begins

> Seek ye first the kingdom of God, and His righteousness; and all these things shall be added unto you. Take therefore no thought for the morrow: for the morrow shall take thought for the things of itself. Sufficient unto the day is the evil thereof."
>
> Matthew 6:33–34, KJV

> God is not limited by environment, family background or present circumstances. God is only limited by our lack of faith.
>
> Osteen, *Your Best Life Now* [13]

July 6, 2005.
The phone rang. It was my dad. He was an emotional train wreck.

"Helen's very sick, Liz." he said, his voice quivering. I had never heard that tone in his voice.

The doctors had given my stepmother, Helen, a twenty percent chance of surviving the next twenty-four hours. What was thought to be the stomach flu had, in reality, been a bowel obstruction. Helen had collapsed and was rushed to the E.R. By this time, she had aspirated into her lungs and gone into septic shock (her body was being poisoned by toxins). Helen was now on full life support. Her kidneys had also shut down and she had been put on dialysis.

My first response was, "Nothing is too big for God, dad—*nothing.*"

Choking back tears, he said, "You're the first person I called because I knew you would say that. I needed to hear that." The seed was already taking root. The Holy Spirit was ministering to dad in his time of need.

Maturing as a Witness

For the past four years, I had been sharing bits of faith with my dad as the opportunities presented themselves. It's more difficult to witness to our family members than to anyone else. I suppose we're most afraid of rejection and condemnation from those that we are closest to. And I know I'm speaking for most of us when I say there is usually enough emotional/psychological baggage between immediate family members to stop a freight-train in its tracks.

But on this day, I knew the seeds had been planted and the Lord had been preparing both of our hearts "for such a time such as this" (Esther 4:14).

The next few months were nerve-wracking. Helen's life hung in the balance between surgeries, infections, respiratory disease, and finally, swelling of the brain. Time and time again, prayers from Oklahoma to Atlanta went out for Helen. Each time she rallied, but at times, we were just mentally and emotionally exhausted. The whole experience was a roller coaster ride that seemingly had no end.

On several occasions the doctors and attending nurses told us that Helen wasn't going to make it, that it would take a miracle to pull her through, to bring her back to any semblance of what she was prior to this medical nightmare. And time after time, God answered our prayers. This left the medical personnel dumbfounded. But to Believers, who pray and believe, it was very simple, very clear—God is good and his word did not return void.

> So shall my word be that goeth forth out of my mouth; it shall not return to me void, but it shall accomplish that which I please and it shall prosper in the thing whereto I sent it.
>
> Isaiah 56:11, KJV

Every time Helen bounced back, my dad took a step closer to renewing his faith. Time and again, he espoused the power of prayer and credited my church, my friends, and business associates with praying Helen through.

The seed was taking root. I was so excited for him and took every opportunity to water that seed with more prayer and encouragement. I had always known that my dad attended Sunday school as a child, but when he began to quote John 3:16 and a few other scriptures, I was blown away. "I know my Scripture. I'm not that far off base," he said jovially, adding: "Train a child in the way he should go: and when he is old he will not depart from it" (Proverbs 22:6). We laughed together as though he had just pulled a rabbit out of a hat. Inside, I was asking, "Okay, where has this man been all my life?"

God Shows His Strength in Our Weakness

Finally, in mid-September, a breakthrough—Helen finally opened her eyes and began to respond ever so slightly. Praise God! Then baby step by baby step, she progressed. Finally, she was able to breathe without the vent. By mid-October, she was discharged from I.C.U. and admitted to the Respiratory Wing.

Shortly thereafter, during an anointed healing service at my church, I stood in for Helen, asking the Lord to heal her throat. If she could not redevelop those muscles, she would not be able to cough or swallow. She would be stuck with a tracheotomy and feeding tube, and institutionalized for the rest of her life. During a powerful prayer, Pastor Mike laid his hands on my throat and said,

"There it is. It's done." And trust me readers, when the Holy Spirit says it's done, *it's done.*

I hurried home after church to call my dad. I told him about the service and how Pastor Mike had prayed for him and Helen, and our whole family.

I said, "Dad, I'm going to step out in faith and say that Helen will have that tracheotomy removed by the end of the week."

"You think so?" he replied, with cautious optimism.

"I know so," I answered.

Praise God, not three days later, the tracheotomy was removed. Halleluiah! Helen's oxygenation levels had reached their optimum and she was finally able to cough up her phlegm on her own. The first post–I.C.U. hurdle had been cleared. According to the specialists and nurses, this development came totally out of the blue. But we knew differently. That which we had prayed for, and claimed in Jesus name, had been given (John 16:23, paraphrased).

The difference in my dad's voice was like night and day. He sounded like a little kid at Christmas time when he relayed the awesome news. "Praise the Lord!" he said. It was the first time I had ever heard him use these words. We both shouted for joy, praising what the Lord had done.

My dad had watched his beloved wife suffer hour after hour, day after day for months, in and out of comas, coughing her insides out non-stop for weeks at a time. And finally, the little bit of faith he had allowed to well up within himself was beginning to pay off. He had humbled himself and asked for prayer time and time again. And God had revealed himself over and over again. It was obvious that He was revealing the awesome truth that "His strength is made perfect in our weakness" (2 Corinthians 12:9).

Dad shared with me that he and Helen had fallen into a rut (as we all do from time to time). Now, in his saddest of moments, he would say things like, "All I want is to be able to sit on the couch again with Helen and hold her hand, and talk. That's *all* I want." Again, he was demonstrating humility, and I just knew God was listening in on those statements.

During the toughest of times, when I couldn't be there physically with him, I would tell him, "Dad, when it gets to the point where you just can't take it anymore, I want you to meditate on this scripture: 'I can do all things through Christ who strengthens me'" (Philippians 4:13, paraphrased).

When Helen had stared death in the face several times, and beaten the odds during her stay in I.C.U., I was compelled by the Holy Spirit to share with him: "God has begun a good work in you and Helen. And he will be well able to bring it to full completion" (Philippians 1:6 paraphrased). I explained to him that God had heard him singing His praises to Helen's family members, the doctors and the nurses. He had been testifying to the power of prayer after each miracle took place in the I.C.U. And because God is a good and faithful God, He was not about to drop he and Helen on their heads.

"God is not in the business of pulling the rug out from beneath a new Believer's feet," I assured him. "I really believe this whole episode will be brought full circle. Helen will recover but it will take time."

Breaking the Generational Curse

At times we would talk about how in every tragedy there were opportunities for growth, lessons to be learned. I explained to my father that he was being pruned in the area of patience. This was a particularly painful pruning for a man who battles depression and anxiety during the best of times.

I also shared with him my belief that our family suffered from a generational curse: the belief taught to us as kids that if we don't ever expect anything good, if we don't dare to hope, then we will never be hurt or disappointed. He whole-heartedly agreed with me.

Oh what a destructive belief that is! And how great a foothold it gives the enemy! Meyer describes the catastrophic effects of this belief system so perfectly, that I cried the first time I read it:

> Some people are afraid to hope because they have been hurt so much
> in life. They have had so many disappointments they don't think
> they can face the pain of another one. Therefore, they refuse to hope

so they won't be disappointed....This type of behavior sets up a negative lifestyle. Everything becomes negative because the thoughts
are negative. [14]

I admitted to dad that that stronghold was the toughest one for me
to overcome in terms of learning to rely on God. And I still struggle
with it from time to time. For as Proverbs 23:7 reminds us, "For as he
thinketh in is heart, so is he" (KJV). What we needed to work on, I
told him, was swapping that negative "stinkin' thinkin'" for a whole
new philosophy that Pastor Mike always stresses: "Expect to receive!
To receive, expect!"

In Matthew 8:13, Jesus heals the centurion's slave, rewarding him
for his faith, saying, "...as thou hast believed, so it be done unto thee"
(KJV). Because the Lord wants us to come to him, to expect good
things from him, to *know* that he is our *loving, faithful Father:*

> Yet the Lord longs to be gracious to you; he rises to show you com-
> passion. For the Lord is a God of justice. Blessed are all who wait
> for him!
>
> Isaiah 30:18

That's a pretty tough sell to someone who has conditioned themselves not to hope, not to ask for anything or expect anything good
to happen. But sell it to ourselves we must if we are ever to form a
deeper relationship with God. We have to learn to trust, because
without trust, there is no relationship.

And from where does this trust issue originate? Talk to somebody
with a trust issue and I'll show you someone who struggles with fear.
Pastor Larry Huch described the generational curse of fear in detail
during his December 4, 2005 TBN television broadcast:
(Paraphrased)

> We need to release ourselves from the curse that keeps us from joy
> in our relationship with God. Fear originated in the Garden of Eden
> when Adam and Eve believed in Satan's lies over God's word. And

we know that the Devil is the father of all lies. When we listen to the liar, we become afraid of what God is telling us.

Fear creates the negative. A curse is put on, taken on, inherited. Unless there are promises of God's blessings, there is a curse causing the problem. Poverty and sickness do not come from God. There is a curse causing the sickness. There are fifteen spirits of fear in the Bible. Fear is the faith that something bad is going to happen. That fear keeps us from trusting God. The spirit of fear is a demonic force. Our heart is our door and fear is a knock at the door. [15]

So, we can either answer that knock and speak and think the negative, creating a self-fulfilled prophecy as Job initially did:

What I feared has come upon me; what I dreaded has happened to me. I have no peace, no quietness; I have no rest, but only turmoil.

Job 3:25–26, NIV

Or, we can "cast down every imagination that exalts itself over the word of God" (2 Corinthians 10:4–5 paraphrased).

One of the most powerful pieces of scripture rebuking fear that I constantly use is found in 2 Timothy 1:7 (KJV):

For God hath not given us a spirit of fear; but of power, and of love, and of a sound mind.

Again, we must expect to receive (Isaiah 30:16)! If you're struggling with the trust issue, you need to turn the *fear factor* on its head. Remember: "without faith it is impossible to please Him" (Hebrews 11:6, KJV). And unless we consistently stay in the word, it is impossible to have faith: "Faith comes from hearing the message, and the message is heard through the word of Christ" (Romans 10:17, NIV).

Daily prayer went up to Helen and dad. Even during the darkest of times, Larry and I would assert, my precious congregation and friends would assert, that Helen would be healed and my father would be strengthened. And they were!

Osteen encourages us to "dare to believe for greater things," to switch our focus from the trials of the natural to the glory and joy of the supernatural:

> "(Hope) has to be conceived in your heart. Look at life through the eyes of faith into that invisible world and see your dreams coming to pass…'Faith is the substance of things hoped for, the evidence of things not seen.' (Hebrews 11:1, KJV). You may not be able to perceive anything positive happening in your life with your natural eyes today.…You may have all kinds of problems, and in the natural order, it doesn't look as though anything is turning around. But don't be discouraged. Look into the invisible world, and through your eyes of faith, see the situation turning around. See your joy and peace being restored. [16]

A Double Portion:
Yet Another Curse is Broken

Still, another curse was plaguing my father: a curse that was based in anxiety over finances. Growing up during the Depression era, during a time when food and shelter were elusive at times, a great insecurity had taken root in my dad. Even though he lives a comfortable lifestyle, he constantly worries about "the bottom falling out."

There came a point in Helen's treatment and recovery, that my father had a choice to make. Realistically, although he wanted to be, he couldn't be with his wife 24/7. Unfortunately, the care that Helen was receiving in the hospital was sub-standard to the point that her life was endangered unless someone was constantly by her side.

If Helen was going to improve, if she was going to *survive,* dad was going to have to hire private nurses to be with Helen around the clock. It was so hard for me not to constantly be there with him. The guilt was almost insufferable. Miss Shirley and I prayed for the Lord to send the right people my dad's way.

Again, He proved Himself to be an "on-time" God. The nursing agency ended up sending two of the most nurturing, capable nurses to care for Helen during this very crucial time. They were sisters, and they each worked twelve-hour shifts to care for Helen.

I am convinced that had God not sent them, Helen would not be alive today. Not only did they nurture her, they were vigilant in making sure that Helen received everything she needed medically to survive this very critical period in her recovery. They basically brought her back from a catatonic state, to a thriving, coherent human being who was able to interact with others again. It was also while Helen was under their care that she was able to have the breathing tube removed.

But private nursing is very expensive. Dad was going to have to ease up on those purse strings to give Helen what she needed, what she deserved, to survive and thrive. It cost him $50,000 but it was worth every cent. I later discussed with dad that I felt that God had given him a test, and he had passed. He had let go of his phobia about money. He had placed love above financial security and the Lord had blessed both he and Helen. This principle is evident in the following Scripture:

> One man gives freely, yet gains more; another withholds unduly, but comes to poverty. A generous man will prosper; he who refreshes others will himself be refreshed...Whoever trusts in his riches will fall, but the righteous will thrive like a green leaf.
>
> Proverbs 11:24–25, 28, NIV

Due to the improvement in care, Helen's condition continued to improve physically, mentally, and emotionally. As a result, she and dad were able to reconnect as a couple, enjoying a deeper relationship, a deeper appreciation for each other, than ever before. *Praise Jesus!*

Deliverance: A *Third* Portion!

Then, another incredible healing took place. This time, the Lord reached out to touch my dad in a very special and miraculous way. I had prayed over the turbulent months for my dad to be delivered from the vice of alcohol. As long as he used the alcohol as a crutch, he would not be able to cope with the demands of the situation.

Unfortunately, my sister and I were not living nearby, and Helen's family members did what they could, but had heavy demands on their lives as well. Night after night, dad would return to an empty house. And night after night, he would rationalize that the whiskey and the beer were helping him relax after a stressful day at the hospital.

The enemy used that lie to rob my father of his inner strength, peace and joy. Inevitably, the next day, he would end up a nervous, irritable and an anxious mess. He was of no use to Helen, or himself for that matter.

Then the moment of *truth* came. He woke up one morning and heard that "still small voice" (1 Kings 19:11, KJV); the whisper we hear when the Holy Spirit convicts us during those quiet moments–the moments when our heart is softened and our spirit is humbled. "You've got two choices," the Holy Spirit said.

"Actually, I only have one choice," my dad replied. "I have to look after Helen. I'm all she has." From that moment on, any psychological or physical craving for alcohol left him! Praise God!

Speaking from experience, I had previously explained to him that sometimes the Lord has to isolate us in order to deal with us. Sometimes we have to be *completely alone* in our tragic circumstance before we can drop our pride and look to Him for comfort and answers. That's what had happened to dad in his bedroom in the quiet hours of the morning.

Not long after, the Lord used one of dad's neighbors, Bill, to hammer home the point that what happened to him was, indeed, supernatural. Bill is a recovering alcoholic. He leaned into my dad's car window one day as he was leaving to go to the hospital, and said, "I can't get over it. I had the shakes and the sweats for three years after I quit drinking. You quit, and that was it! I don't get it!"

But I "get it," and now my dad "gets it," too. During one of our phone calls when he relayed this conversation to me, I told him, "Dad, it's a 'God thing.' He delivered you from alcohol. That's exactly how He did it for me as well."

"Yeah, I think it had to be," he agreed.

It was a double blessing! Not only had my dad quit drinking, he had given credit to God for it! Praise the Lord and pass the Sprite!

Today, he is several months clean and sober and able to handle life's situations with a new-found strength and confidence he has never had before.

Today, Helen is in a rehabilitation center in Toronto. My dad makes the two-hour round trip to visit and look after her five days a week. He would never have been able to do that if he had not been delivered from alcohol. Helen is working very hard to improve her physical strength so that she and dad can be together again soon in an assisted living community. In addition to her regular physical therapy, dad acts as her personal trainer, assisting her with her weight training with dumb bells. They go for long walks outside; dad pushing Helen in her wheelchair.

It's been a year and a half since Helen was first hospitalized, but she has continued to "fight the good fight." And Glory to God, Helen and dad recently became hooked on Joyce Meyer's television show, *Enjoying Your Everyday Life.*

Touched by Katrina

Not two months after my step-mother was hospitalized, my husband's family would be affected by Hurricane Katrina, the monstrous storm that struck New Orleans in September of 2005. Larry's family lives on what is known as "the West Bank" of New Orleans. When the storm struck, Larry's mom (affectionately known as Mema) was living with his sister and brother-in-law.

They initially fled to Alabama and were riding out the storm in a small hotel room. Mema is in poor health and was in need of regular medical care. She needed a stable environment. So, within a few days of the storm hitting, Mema came to live with us.

As much as you love a family member, there is always an adjustment period involved when the family dynamic is altered. Jake, who has always been an only child, had to learn to share his mother's attention. Mema had to get used to the constant activity of a family with a young child. And I was thrown even deeper into the role of the "sandwich generation." Not only was I dealing with the crisis in Canada, I had become the main care giver for Larry's mom—all while balancing my roles as a mother, wife and newly-contracted author. To say I was a little stressed would be a gross understatement...

While my mother-in-law posed a bundle of new responsibilities, she was also a great help to me—helping out with household chores and watching over Jake when I would have to rest because of my back pain.

But the enemy was tugging at me, big time. Old feelings of frustration and resentment began to plague me. Beginning at the age of eight and coming in various forms, it seemed as if I had always had unusual amounts of responsibility placed on me. It was all finally coming to a head. Old issues between Larry and I regarding responsibility began to resurface. So now there was stress on my marriage as well. It was becoming harder and harder to control my tongue.

Under normal circumstances, I might have had more patience, but I was dealing with so many other issues at the time, that my patience was being stressed to the maximum. And, in all honesty, I was battling the family curse of impatience, depression and anxiety.

At first, I perceived all of these challenges to be obstacles, trials that were getting in the way of completing this project for God. At one point, I was giving the enemy credit for dissuading me from completing the mission to spread the Gospel.

My flesh wanted to get all twisted up in knots, to complain to the point where I couldn't stand myself. I prayed constantly, asking God to forgive me for my sour attitude and my negative thoughts, to give me the strength and peace I needed to complete the book for His glory.

Then, it came as it always does, supernaturally–that peace that surpasses all understanding. Once I turned the situation over to the Lord, believing that if I did the right things (looking after my father, step-mother and mother-in-law in their time of need...*with a righteous attitude*) that He would work all things out for my good and His glory (Romans 8:28 paraphrased).

Then slowly, the stress would begin to wear on me, exhaustion would kick in, peace would dissipate, and the heaviness would return.

I had to trust that the Lord was in control; that the book would be completed according to His timetable, not mine. Over and over I prayed, "Father, I just have to believe that there is a good reason for all of these trials to arise at the same time." And then, boom, out of nowhere, Jesus would lift the veil of frustration and anxiety that was distorting my perspective. I could view these trials as obstacles or as experiences meant to enrich the quality of the book's message.

It was during this time that I picked up Osteen's National Best Seller, *Your Best Life Now*. The third Chapter discusses how we need to break the barriers of the past if we ever want to *enlarge the vision for our lives and receive God's favor*. Again, my battle against the family curse was revealed and confirmed:

> God will help you break that curse in your family, but it will take perseverance and a willingness to change on your part....Maybe nobody in your family ever really took God at His word. Break through those barriers of the past. This is a new day, and God wants to do a new thing. Enlarge your vision. Stretch your faith. You can be the first. You can be the one to "raise the bar." If you believe, all things are possible. [17]

If I was going to complete this book, fulfill my vision, I was going to have to break the curse. I was going to have to "raise the bar" and believe all things are possible.

During the most difficult of times, I would respond to alter calls at church, seeking prayer. I asked the Lord to quell the negativity. The bitterness, anxiety, old habits and attitudes that were resurfacing, threatened to undermine the peace that God intended for me and my family.

On one occasion, Jeff, an associate pastor, prophesied over me. "I see a garbage can being kicked over," he said. "Old attitudes are being kicked over, gotten rid of."

He had hit the nail right on the head. As mentioned earlier, a truly anointed, genuine prophesy strictly confirms what a person already knows in his heart. It was up to me to eradicate those old thoughts and feelings because those two channels are the enemy's way in. We cannot give him a foothold in any area. It's a constant struggle, a battle we must forge and win on a daily basis.

That's not to say, that I didn't struggle from time to time—I'm human. But if the foundation of faith is there, you can rebuke the enemy's attacks and pray yourself out of the pit...even if it feels like it's inch by inch sometimes. And the only way to do that is to soothe the soul with His Word. Without the Word, we continue on in the spiritual wasteland, caught in the mire of despair.

So I prayed and prayed, meditating on scripture regarding the power of the tongue. Frustration and irritability were hampering my ability to write. God was feeling farther and farther away.

How could I write this inspirational book when I was facing such a spiritual battle myself? Again, I prayed constantly, and begged the Lord and my family for forgiveness when I gave in to the destructive power of my tongue. For we know, "the tongue has the power of life and death" (Proverbs 18:21, NIV), and the former was becoming more prominent than the latter. The Bible tells us that when we are under stress, we are more vulnerable to temptation (Mark 14:38), and there were times I would give in to the temptation to speak "guile." The desire to change was there, but I needed the Holy Spirit's intervention.

The Holy Spirit Shows Up...Just In Time!

With just a few months before deadline, it was becoming painfully clear that I was going to have to ask my publisher for an extension. The year since I had signed my contract had flown by.

Concerned about how my publisher might react, I went up for alter call during revival services at church in April. The enemy had also been pressing on me once again with the fear of a recurrence with cancer. Many symptoms related to stress were popping up, challenging my faith that "He would complete the work He had begun in me" (Philippians 1:6).

An awesome evangelical couple, Pastor Will and Alicia Hardy, were visiting our church that weekend. On Friday night, I asked Pastor Mike to pray for me concerning my desire to win the battle within my mind: I needed to overcome the anxiety and depression I felt myself slipping into. I needed to complete the work that the Lord had for me, and I couldn't do it if my energy and my mind weren't focused. Pastor Mike prayed over me, prophesying that he saw at least four other books sitting on a shelf waiting to be completed.

The following night, I asked Pastor Hardy to pray over me concerning all of the obstacles that had come my way since signing the contract for the book, and that I was concerned about asking for an extension on my deadline. In confirmation of Pastor Mike's prophecy, the young, but powerful, evangelist also envisioned that not only would I complete this book, but that at least *four or five others* were in my future. "Don't be frustrated by deadlines," he told me. "God can write a book in a day."

That statement stuck with me throughout the rest of the writing process. I took the Holy Spirit's words to heart. When situations kept me from writing, I remembered these words and kept frustration at bay. In doing so, I was able to enjoy the little things in life, the precious moments, despite a looming deadline and a mountain of responsibility.

And, not coincidentally, I found it particularly intriguing that neither man knew that I had *four or five* other books in mind to complete following this project. God is good...all the time.

In addition, during this revival period, I received further healing in my back and legs. Glory to God, the pain lessened to a degree that I kept forgetting to take my medication!

I could no longer put off asking for an extension. I wrote to Dr. Richard Tate (founder of Tate Publishing and Enterprises, LLC) and explained my situation. The class act that he is, and with an attitude of graciousness, he immediately granted me a *six-month* extension. I will always be grateful for that.

Reading and praying continually, I asked Jesus to relieve me of the mind-binding spirits that were hampering my relationships and the progress of the book. Finally, I literally *got on my face* on the carpet beside my bed. I poured out my heart and sought His face, crying and repenting for all the weaknesses I had exhibited during the previous months.

And the battle continued for control of my tongue. As mentioned earlier, it's a well-known fact that women tend to develop the use of their tongue when they feel threatened, versus men who develop their brawn. I looked up every scripture that dealt with that issue and vowed to overcome my weakness. If anyone has fought that fight, you know how challenging it is.

A Time of Refreshing

In May of 2006, Mema returned to New Orleans for a couple of months to visit family, friends and her church. Her time away would be a time for regrouping for me and my family. It would also provide more time for me to read scripture and dig myself out of the spiritual hole I was in. God had provided a second wind. The past ten months had put quite a strain on our family. As my counselor reassured me, even Jesus needed time alone to refuel–escaping from the crowds, and even His own disciples, once in a while.

Many of the sermons during this time period seemed to speak directly to the issues my family was facing (it's funny the way God arranges that...). I hungered for His word. I was desperate to eradicate what felt like a demonic presence that was seeking to destroy my family and my vision.

I wanted to be more Christ-like. I reached out to God as never before. I re-read one of my favorite books in the Bible, the *Book of Ruth*. Even before I was a Christian, I was drawn to that story. My heart's desire: to pursue the same sort of godly relationship with Mema that Ruth and Naomi had dedicated themselves to. I prayed and prayed, meditating again on the Scripture regarding the power of the tongue.

Most of the time, I believe I provided a loving atmosphere for Mema; there were periods when I allowed my frustration to peek through. Lying on the floor in my office, I repented for my lack of control over my tongue and my negative thoughts and feelings. I called Mema in New Orleans and asked her for her forgiveness. She graciously gave it to me.

Speaking To the Mountains

Pastor Hardy and his wife, Alicia returned to our church. The message that day touched me so deeply that I returned to the alter (aren't there seasons in our life when the alter is our best friend?). I completely broke down sobbing, surrendering my heart to the Lord, and asking Him to cleanse me of all unrighteousness. I felt as though the enemy was pursuing me, trying to discredit the work that the Lord had given me, and the opportunity that He had blessed me with.

Asking the Pastor and his wife to pray for me, I explained my emotional dilemma that I needed to be freed from. I told them that it almost felt as though I was battling a demon within, and I needed to be cleansed. I was not only hurting others, I was hurting myself and disappointing God.

I shared with them that when I was initially born again, I promised God that if He healed me of cancer, that I would raise Jake to be a good, strong, Christian man. Part of that promise included not only surrounding him with Christian environments at school and at church, but also at home.

I battled nagging doubts within me as to whether or not I was presenting a Godly example to my child. After all, Larry and I are going to be Jake's paramount examples in life. I wanted to be sure that I could fulfill that promise to the Lord and to Jake.

And, as God would arrange it, Alicia was the perfect person to pray for me. She too had struggled with these same difficulties. Together we prayed for a healing of the mind, to be freed from the mind-binding spirit and the generational curses that plagued me. For we know that the mind is the gateway to the heart and that "above all else [we must] guard our heart, for it is the well-spring of life" (Proverbs 4:23, NIV). If our heart is struggling, our words will reflect that.

I was exhausted after the service. The following morning, I felt a cleansing that I had for so long desired. As shown in the stories within this book, the Lord always sends just the right people at just the right to time to help you with your Christian walk.

In my time of struggle, I had turned to the Lord and He had

provided. Now it was my turn to bless others as I had been blessed. As God promised Abraham in Genesis 12:2, "I will bless you...and you will be a blessing" (NIV). I concentrated on those old familiar promises that had gotten me over the previous mountains I had to climb with Jesus at my side:

> Philippians 1:6 (NIV): "...being confident about this, that He who began a good work in you will carry it on to completion until the day of Christ Jesus."

> Jeremiah 29:11–13: "...For I know the plans I have for you," declares the Lord, "plans to prosper you and not to harm you, plans to give you hope and a future. Then you will call upon me and come and pray to me, and I will listen to you. You will seek me and find me when you seek me with all your heart. I will be found by you and bring you back from captivity."

Those scriptures came alive to me as never before. What was a life-jacket to me during my battle with cancer and paralysis had become a lifeboat during this season of strife. As did the women in this book, I became convinced of the truth found in Hebrews 13:8: "Jesus Christ is the same yesterday, today and tomorrow." He is consistent and we have to strive for the same "Christ-like" consistency. There are times when we have to rededicate our hearts and minds to Him.

God Calls Us to "Camp JAM"— A Tsunami of Salvation

In June, we had the opportunity to serve the Lord by volunteering to be counselors at "Camp JAM" (Jesus and Me); a three-day retreat for the kids in our church age 8 -18. "Camp JAM" is the same camp headed up by Christy as described in "Christy's Story." At first, I struggled with the idea of whether or not I should take time away from writing to do this. But after praying about it, I knew that this would be an incredible opportunity to serve the Lord by ministering to children.

I remembered Pastor Hardy's words re: "God can write a book in a day." I listened to God's will above all else, not getting hung up on deadlines and missing out on other opportunities for ministry. I could have sent Larry and Jake off to camp and used those four days to write, but The Master Planner was at work as usual! Despite everything, He would make sure that our family made it to camp to fulfill yet another mission for Him.

It was hard to see His hand at work at the time. Not only was I concerned about the deadline; as the enemy would have it, I had been experiencing some physical manifestations of the stress I was under. I had had tests run by my gynecologist to rule out the recurrence of cancer and had visited the gastroenterologist. My oncologist had scheduled a CT scan, and of course, the date for the scan landed just two days before we were to leave for camp.

That old fear of "what if the cancer is back," started to creep in. I fought it to the best of my ability. Some days were better than others. The date was getting closer. I had to make a decision. Sermons on healing, faith and fear bolstered my "what if" battle.

Then, one morning while praying and searching the scriptures for wisdom regarding the choice I had to make, the Holy Spirit was faithful as always. He led me to Mark 9:36–37:

> He took a little child and had him stand among them. Taking him in his arms, He said to [the disciples], "Whoever welcomes one of these little children in my name welcomes me; and whoever welcomes me does not welcome me but the one who sent me." (NIV)

There was my answer. You know it when you can feel it in your soul: that truth that strikes at your heart, giving you that inexplicable peace.

I could either spend that week picking up the absolutely horrible tasting contrast from my doctor in Atlanta, swallowing said foul substance, sliding through the CT tube and then wait on pins and needles for the results…or I could continue writing, and then serve the Lord at Camp JAM. All the while, I meditated on His command to "(…walk by faith and not by sight)" (2 Corinthians 5:7, KJV). I claimed His promise to give me a long life and show me salvation (Psalm 91:14–16, KJV, paraphrased). Satan was not going to steal my family's joy in our call to service.

The decision was made: if there was something wrong, it would have to wait until after camp. I rescheduled the CT scan. I was not going to let fear prevent me from serving the Lord. I had to answer the burning desire to "be about my father's business" (Luke 2:49).

More importantly, "I knew that I knew that I knew" that if I was, in fact sick, if God were to call me home, I would stand before Him, and He would say, "Well done, my good and faithful servant. Well done." I concluded that I'd rather be a faithful servant than a fearful one. I meditated constantly on 2 Timothy 1:7 (KJV), "For God hath not given us a spirit of fear, but of power, love and a sound mind."

If I was going to break through this spiritual bondage, I was going to have to claim my healing and rebuke the fear.

Emily Dotson discusses the importance of consistently claiming our healing in her article entitled, "Use God's Word as Your Healing Foundation, Or You Will Take on Deception." Dotson, herself, was supernaturally healed of lupus. By claiming God's healing scriptures in 1983, she "brought [herself] back from death's door from the last stages of lupus."

Citing Hebrews 4:14, Dotson explains that "[for] Jesus to act on professions, we must profess, or confess His Word."

> "Therefore, since we have a great high priest who has gone through the heavens, Jesus the Son of God, let us hold firmly to the faith we profess." (KJV)

Since 2001, I had been battling what Dotson describes as the enemy's "[deceptive] pain symptoms."

> "However, symptoms can't change God's Covenant promise. If they could, we would all be in trouble. But…'God is not a man that he should lie; neither the son of man, that he should repent: Hath he said, and shall He not do it? Or hath he spoken, and shall he not make it good?'(Numbers, 23:19, KJV). By Jeremiah, we have an everlasting covenant with God; He will not turn away from us;…
>
>   Jeremiah, 32:40, KJV

…We cannot afford to slack up on our faith and Word confessions when the attack is still coming. If we do, our mind is wide open for Satan to deceive us when he turns up the pain symptoms.

...the devil will not be able to deceive us or take from us what Jesus has provided through the power of the Cross.

...Good health is worth all the effort of fighting the faith battle. Laziness will take you to the grave." [18]

I had meditated on the healing scriptures, and claimed my body to be whole and healthy. I had finally *had enough!* I was finished with the scans, tests, and doctor appointments! Two of my doctors wanted to perform various procedures and surgeries. As I continued to pray and study scripture, the Lord spoke to me and pierced my soul:

For thou hast delivered my soul from death, mine eyes from tears, and my feet from falling. I will walk before the Lord in the land of the living. I believed, therefore I have spoken: I was greatly afflicted: I said in my haste, All men are liars.

Psalms 116: 8–11, KJV

Don't get me wrong, I am not accusing the doctors of being liars. I *am* accusing Satan of being the king of lies, and provoking the symptoms for the doctors to respond to.

Determined to *live my life* and *fulfill my vision,* my *mission for God,* I became vigilant in rebuking Satan's influence over my body. After five long years, I had *finally won the battle!* Satan could no longer torture me through a fear of recurrence. Praise God, there is victory in the Word!

I was going to ignore the "deceptive pain symptoms" and minister to the kids at Camp JAM. However, the enemy is persistent and he wasn't through with me on this one. If he can't come through the front door, he'll try to sneak in the back: "What do *you have* to offer those kids?" he whispered in my ear. "You're struggling with your *own faith* right now. God can't possibly use *you* in the state you're in!"

As Pastor Mike always says, "Liar, liar pants on fire!" Shaking off the encroaching doubts, I began packing my family up for Camp JAM. And what an awesome time in the Lord we had! It was an experience that Larry, Jake and I will forever treasure. The Holy Spirit *moved us* and *used us* in so many ways that weekend! We were so blessed by the kids as they responded to teachings, testimonies and the unconditional love that was imparted to them.

Then, it happened...on the third night of Camp JAM, during praise and worship, the Holy Spirit fell and moved in a way many of us had never seen before. You could hand me a million dollars and I wouldn't trade it for what I witnessed that night. And God *had* used me to help bring it about. Thank you, Jesus! Don't get me wrong, God would have found a way to bring it about with or without me. But, had I listened to the enemy, and not gone to camp, I would never have received the blessing of witnessing an awesome movement of the Lord. More than seventy children were either saved or were baptized by the Holy Spirit!

Here's how it all unfolded: earlier that day, I was preparing to make tie-dye t-shirts with the teenagers. The theme for camp activities that day was to help the kids explore who they *were* in Christ and who they wanted *to be* in Christ.

As I prayed and asked the Holy Spirit for guidance as to how I could reach out to the teens in such a way that would melt their "I'm too cool to listen" attitude, the Holy Spirit responded: "Before you utter a word, before you begin to teach on this message, I want you to play the song, 'Who Am I.'"

"But tie-dye is so time-consuming," I replied, "and if I play the song first, we might not have time to finish."

"Play the song," replied the Holy Spirit. When the Holy Spirit repeats Himself, you know you've received confirmation. Despite the time constraints, I was going to play the song.

I was familiar with this contemporary Christian song but could not remember the name of the group that sang it. Frantically, I searched through all of my CD's, but to no avail. There were only a few minutes left before the teens would arrive at my station. Praise God, my assistant, Megan, remembered that the contemporary Christian band, *Casting Crowns*, sang it and that one of the other assistants, Danielle, had the CD. Running around like frantic little chickens, we were able to get the CD just in time. I wasn't sure at the time as to whether or not the song spoke to the kids, but later that night we found out that it *did.*

Praise and worship began after dinner as the sun began to set on our humble little camp site. As one of the counselors played guitar and sang, one of the teenage girls approached me and asked me if I still had the *Casting Crowns* CD containing "Who Am I." She retrieved it from Danielle and then asked Christy if she and two other girls could sing the song for the rest of the kids. Christy approved, the CD was cued, and the girls began to sing:

Who am I, that the Lord of all the earth
Would care to know my name,
Would care to feel my hurt?
Who am I, that the Bright and Morning Star
Would choose to light the way
For my ever wandering heart?

Not because of who I am,
But because of what You've done.
Not because of what I've done,
But because of who You are.

I am Yours.
Whom shall I fear?
Whom shall I fear?
'Cause I am Yours.
I am Yours...[19]

While the girls sang, Van (one of the counselors) began to walk through the crowd: "Come on everyone! Get up on your feet!" he encouraged them. "Raise your hands up and praise Him!"

Before the girls could get half way through the song, the kids began to approach our make-shift alter, one after the other, asking to be saved or just sobbing, not knowing how to describe what they were feeling.

The first little boy, Jonah, his hands raised, tears streaming down his face, could barely breathe. Some of the other children led the nine-year-old to the front to Christy. "My heart is burning! My heart is burning!" he said. "Don't be afraid, Jonah," Christy said, tears flowing down her cheeks by this time. "It's just the Holy Spirit." She began to pray the prayer of salvation over him.

Seconds later, I noticed another little boy, coming toward me, in the same state as the rest of the kids. He was crying so hard, he couldn't speak, and his hands were raised as he worshipped the Lord. I quickly took him to alter where Christy and the other camp counselors were still praying over Jonah as he received the baptism of the Holy Spirit. He would receive salvation just moments later.

The flood continued. Eight-year-old Jacie came alongside me, sobbing, also unable to speak. "Just raise your hands and worship Him, Jacie! Just worship Him!" I said. I knew that Jacie had been saved and baptized, so I lead her to alter as well to receive the Holy Spirit.

Nothing could have prepared me for what was occurring at that moment. The majority of the kids were also speaking in tongues! Within minutes, the entire audience made their way to alter in what looked like a *tsunami* of salvation. A wave of approximately seventy kids praised the Lord with every ounce of faith they had. The Holy Spirit had fallen in a way that I can only describe as a "mini-Pentecost." It was breath-taking.

Stepping Out in Faith

That experience reinforced God's word that we must "walk by faith and not by sight" (2 Corinthians 5:7) and obey Him. And when we do, miraculous things can, and *do*, take place. I was honored to witness such an event and to be used by God for His glory.

Once again, the Lord had taught me to focus on faith, overcome my fears, and serve Him. But still, I was confronted with physical symptoms that the doctors felt were cause for concern. In my spirit I knew that I was fine, but Satan continued to try to distract me.

Then one afternoon, as I was driving down the road, the Holy Spirit asked me, "What would you be thinking about right now if you weren't thinking about possible sickness?"

"I'd be thinking about the Lord and what I could be doing for Him," I answered.

The obsessive thought process broke instantly. I felt total peace and more relaxed than I had in months. That's what it means to "cast all our cares onto Him" (1 Peter 5:7). He can take all of our fears and worries so that we can "be about His business." We can know the truth and be set free. We can put our faith and His words into action.

My mind was no longer frozen with distraction. The pathway to the Holy Trinity was re-opened. Peace, like a river, flowed. With this peace, came clarity of vision. Once again, I was able to let go of the past and focus on finishing "my Father's work."

In the third chapter of Philippians, Paul discusses the importance of forgetting the past and reaching toward the goal. He says:

> Brethren, I count not myself to have apprehended: but this one thing
> I do, forgetting those things which are behind, and reaching forth
> unto those things which are before. I press toward the mark for the
> prize of the high calling of God in Christ Jesus (13–14, KJV).

A Second Wind

During the time that my mother-in-law was in New Orleans, Larry, Jake and I had time to go on a couple of short trips and just enjoy "being" together.

I was convinced that when she returned, a rejuvenated spirit would prevail. It did for a while, and then slowly, I could feel that heavy spirit creeping back in. This wasn't just a heavy spirit; it was a *strong* heavy spirit. Then, as always, when the heart's desire is there, when the time is right, God steps in to intervene. And boy, did we need it!

Divine intervention showed up at our dining room table a week after Mema's return. We had invited Pastor Mike and Miss Shirley, Christy and James, and their two children over for dinner.

As Pastor Mike said the blessing, he spoke "peace" over our household. As he uttered "peace," it was as if a calming spirit was emitted from his lips. What I had prayed about and searched the Word for, for several months, finally came to pass.

But what it took was the "effectual and fervent prayer a righteous man" (James 5:16), spoken over a table of people who were gathered in a moment of agreement and love. It was just too much for the enemy. The next morning, peace was granted. There was a new "light-ness" that came to dwell in our home. And it was all in God's timing.

The heaviness, frustration and anger were gone. It was nothing less than a miracle! Praise God! Truth had triumphed over tragedy once again!

It was the beginning of a more peaceful and loving environment in our home. Of course, we all continue to work on our weaknesses. It's a process...but we're all seeking and enjoying a closer walk with Jesus.

Peace is Challenged...Again!

Then...again! Yet another challenge arises! Ally, my now 18-year-old niece asked if she could come to live with us. Her grandparents, who she had been living with, had sold their home, were moving a distance away, and she needed somewhere to stay before she went back to school in January. It was mid-July and my book was due at the end of September.

As mentioned in the first chapter, I adore my niece and love her as a daughter. But Ally was coming from a very secular, if not dark and negative household. Not surprisingly, she was very cynical about, and resistant to, the Christian faith. And the cherry on the cake was that she was also battling *full-blown* bulimia.

For those of you who are unfamiliar with this disease, in its most simple terms, bulimia is an eating disorder characterized by binge eating followed by purging. This disease is hell to live with, for both the afflicted person and the people surrounding her. It takes its toll, physically, mentally, emotionally, and financially.

Bulimia is an addiction. But the bulimic is addicted to food and the euphoric release they feel when they purge. And like any other addict, the bulimic will look you straight in the eye and lie to continue in their addictive lifestyle. If Ally were an alcoholic or drug addict, it would be a no-brainer: there are no drugs or alcohol in our house. But how do you keep your home "food-free" when you have to feed four other people?

So, needless to say, Larry and I were very concerned about Ally and there were many challenges involved in her coming to live with us.

As more people filled our house, the smaller our house became (I know there are others out there who can relate, Amen!). Due to certain circumstances, Ally had not yet gotten her drivers' license, and, of course, she was in need of counseling. She would have to find a job and we would need to finish a room downstairs for her. At the same time, I would also need to get Jake ready for school. As I said at the beginning of this chapter, when it rains, it pours!

It seemed as though our family had just acquired peace over a change in family dynamics, and suddenly, the dynamics were being altered once again! As much as I have always wanted to have Ally to come to live with us, the litany of the things I would be responsible for in helping her get on her feet freaked me out in terms of the book deadline. I had only eight weeks left. I felt myself beginning to panic again; feeling overwhelmed and anxious. I prayed and re-read the Book of James over and over again.

But God is so faithful. One morning, The Holy Spirit whispered: "Stress can either *motivate* you or *debilitate* you: *it's your choice.*" I began to meditate on that powerful phrase. As I meditated, the stronger I felt. The insecurities I had felt about lacking organizational skills and being a strong matriarch (especially under stress) began to melt away. I felt a supernatural peace and energy begin to flow. I would be *motivated,* not intimidated or debilitated!

With this new attitude and approach, God blessed me again. The challenges of having to meet the needs of others in my household turned into an awesome blessing. We all began to pull together in unity. With my mind cleared, I recovered my old abilities to multi-task and delegate responsibilities to others. In addition, Ally and

Mema helped me look after Jake, and that allowed me more time and energy to focus on my writing.

And here's a praise report! After sowing many seeds, the Lord had answered our prayers for my niece. Because of everything she had been through in her eighteen years, Ally was disillusioned with God. From time to time she had softened her heart, but would eventually return to a very dark, cynical outlook.

She had been living with us for about a month by this time, and had attended church a couple of times. On the third visit, a guest evangelist, an elderly gentleman from Augusta, would give the sermon. At first glance, I thought, "Oh no. He's an older gentleman. Ally is probably not going to be able to relate to his message. Why couldn't Pastor Mike have preached today?" I couldn't have been more wrong. During the comical but Bible-based, straight-shooting sermon, Ally leaned over to me and whispered, "I like him." I almost fell off my seat.

In fact, just a couple of weeks before, a younger evangelist had spoken at our church and, for whatever reason, his message did not have the effect on my teenage niece that the older evangelist's did. Go figure. You just never know who God is going to use to minister to your loved ones.

After the pastor had finished his very animated sermon on the importance of choosing eternal life or damnation, he gave an alter call. I looked over at Ally and was surprised to see her eyes were brimming with tears! Glory to God! I asked her if she wanted to go up to the front. She said, no, but that she wanted me to pray for her. I put my arm around her tiny waist and prayed as the congregation prayed the Sinners' Prayer. Ally quietly repeated it. She later asked me, "I don't get it. Why am I crying?"

"That's the Holy Spirit tugging on your heart, babe," I said.

That night, we had an awesome talk about salvation. Ally told me that she was at her happiest several years ago when she was reading the Bible every night. At that time, I had just received salvation and Larry and I were sharing the Gospel with her. "I want to start reading the Bible again," she announced. "I'm going to start tonight." Those were the sweetest words I could have ever heard coming from her mouth. She was taking the first step. She was finally seeking Him again! Praise Jesus!

The real praise report came months later when Ally turned her life over to Christ and received salvation! It happened one Sunday morning when the Holy Spirit told me to stay home from church because Ally needed me. She had just spent several days in a rehabilitation center for women with eating disorders. While there, she had felt a peace come over her. Not coincidently, I received that same peace "that surpasses understanding", confirming that the Holy Spirit was intervening on Ally's behalf. She was finally at peace, and able to kick the bulimic urges while in the hospital.

So on that beautiful Sunday morning, we ended up, sitting on the couch in the family room together, talking about the Lord and salvation. At one point I went into the kitchen to make coffee.

"I really want it, Aunt Liz," Ally announced. "I really want to be saved."

I stopped what I was doing. "So what's stopping you?" I asked.

"Nothing," she said, shrugging her shoulders.

"Let's do it!" I said, barely able to contain myself.

I rushed over to the couch and took her hands in mine. I thanked the Lord for this moment, for the moment our family had prayed for, for years! Not only had she been delivered from the eating disorder, her eternal life was about to be saved! Then we prayed the Prayer of Salvation. And it was so sweet and sincere! Ally was radiant! She was spilling over with excitement and couldn't wait to testify to her friends and the rest of the family! Praise God and Halleluiah!

September, 2006

So, instead of being worn out by the events of the past eighteen months (as the enemy would have it), I am renewed and refreshed; not only within, but more importantly, in my relationships with others. And, *most importantly* I feel closer to Christ than ever. My callings are clearer to me than ever before: I am to be a servant/messenger for God and the matriarch of my household. Put simply, at the age of thirty-nine, it is time to GROW UP! Having matured in the spirit, the spirit was taking care of the natural.

The Lord has made it clear that the many trials I have faced are positives, not negatives. He has used them to re-shape my character. From now on, I will rebuke the temptation to buckle under the pressure and revert to my old habits of dealing with stress. Instead, with God's grace and mercy, I am now equipped to *clear my vision* and *invert my perspective.*

When I turned everything over to Him, I could see that this season of tragedy was giving me the opportunity to deal with my own generational curses while ministering to, and sharing fellowship with, my loved ones. In order to survive this challenging period and complete the book, I would have to delve deeper into the Word and draw closer to God. In the process, I would receive the precious gifts of the rejuvenation of faith and the re-molding of my character through the power of the Holy Spirit! This process is explained so eloquently by Paul in Romans 5:1–5 (NIV):

> Therefore, since we have been justified through faith, we have peace with God through our Lord Jesus Christ, through whom we have gained access by faith into this grace in which we now stand. And we rejoice in the hope of the glory of God, Not only so, but we also rejoice in our sufferings, because we know that suffering produces perseverance; perseverance, character; and character, hope. And hope does not disappoint us because God has poured out his love into our hearts by the Holy Spirit whom he has given us.

And through it all, yet another invaluable lesson was learned: the enemy can steal only what we allow him to steal. From here on out, I claim the following, not just for myself, but for all who are seeking triumph over tragedy:

I claim God's blessings for Job after many years of suffering. In the 42nd chapter of Job it is revealed that the Lord will "make [us] prosperous again and give [us] twice as much as [we] had before" (10). He will "[bless] the latter part of [our lives] more than the first" (12a), and "[we] will die old and full of years" (17).

I claim that God will take our adversity and seeming injustice and turn it around for our good and his glory (Romans 8:28 paraphrased).

I claim that the Lord will restore the years that the enemy has stolen from us. (Joel 2:25a paraphrased)

I claim that the Lord has plans not to harm us, but to prosper us: plans for hope and a future. When we pray to Him, He will hearken to us. When we seek Him with all our hearts, we will find Him (Jeremiah 29:11–13 paraphrased)

I claim that Jesus Christ has already paid the price for our sin! We are covered in the blood of the lamb: "He was wounded for our transgressions; He was bruised for our iniquities: the chastisement of our peace was upon Him; *and with his stripes we are healed.*" (Isaiah 54:5, KJV, emphasis mine)

I claim that we shall *diligently* seek the truth, know the truth, and be set free. (John 8:32)

I claim that we shall not perish, for we shall keep our eyes on the vision before us; God's plan and purpose for our lives.

I claim all of these promises in the name of Jesus, through the power of the Holy Spirit.

As I sit and "peck out" these last words, I realize that I will always remember the past year and a half as one of the most difficult, but most *empowering* times of my life. Yes, I had to walk through the fire (again) to get to where God needed me to be. Although the heat was painful at times, I trusted in the Lord and sought His truth, knowing that He would bring me, and my family, out on the other side.

As Jesus promised, He held my hand all the while, blessing me by replacing what the enemy had tried to steal. The book that I was destined to write for the Lord was complete. *3T Vision* was *finally* a reality, despite the enemy's best efforts to thwart it. In the meantime, the Lord had delivered me and my family through the trials and tragedies and on to triumph!

And when He did, I was a new creature, Praise God. The trials of the previous year had forced me to dig deeper into the Word and crave His presence. Fighting the battles while writing and meditating on the preceding awe-inspiring stories, took me from the "milk" to the "meat" (Hebrews 5).

It wasn't always easy, but the desire to please God kept me holding on, talking to Him, trusting in His truth. The Lord had honed me and shaped me into the woman, *the messenger*, He had intended me to be.

Ouch and Halleluiah!

An Invitation:

Thank you for reading *3T Vision*. I pray that it has touched your heart and inspired you. If you have finished reading this book, and feel lead to make Jesus the Lord of your life, please pray with me:

> Lord Jesus, I ask you to come in to my heart today. I believe that you are the son of God, and that you were born of a virgin. I believe that you were crucified for my sins; that you were resurrected on the third day, and presently sit at the right hand of our Father. I ask you to forgive me of my sins. My heart's desire is to make you my Lord and my Savior.

If you prayed that prayer, you have just become a child of God with royal blood flowing through your veins. He has forgiven your sins and cast them into the sea of forgetfulness. Please stay in the Word and find a good Bible-based church. Today is the first day of the rest of your life with Jesus Christ as your Lord and Savior!

Happy Birthday!

A Final Note:

Throughout each story, the following principle remains clear: No matter what trial, temptation, or tragedy we face, "Jesus Christ is the same yesterday and today and forever" (Hebrews 13:8, NIV). His Father's *truth* is timeless ("The lip of truth shall be established forever."—Proverbs 12:19) and it will *always triumph over tragedy*. With those promises engraved in our hearts, and our "3T Vision" focused solely on Him, we are guaranteed to be "more than conquerors" through Christ Jesus. He will always show up to carry us through the fire and over to the other side where He will set our feet on solid rock.

Additional Scripture

Psalm 116: 1–11 (KJV)
I love the Lord because he hath heard my voice and my supplications.
Because he hath inclined his ear unto me, therefore will I call upon Him as long as I live.
The sorrows of death compassed me, and the pains of hell gat hold upon me: I found trouble and sorrow.
Then called I upon the name of the Lord; O Lord, I beseech thee, deliver my soul. Gracious is the Lord, and righteous; yea, our God is merciful.
The Lord preserveth the simple: I was brought low, and he helped me.
Return unto thy rest, O my soul; for the Lord hath dealt bountifully with thee.
For thou hast delivered my soul from death, mine eyes from tears, and my feet from falling.
I will walk before the Lord in the land of the living.
I believed, therefore have I spoken: I was greatly afflicted:
I said in my haste, All men are liars.

Psalm 118: 1, 5–6, 8, 14–19 *(KJV)*

O give thanks unto the Lord; for he is good: because his mercy *endureth* for ever.

I called upon the Lord in distress: The Lord answered me, and set me in a large place.

The Lord is on my side; I will not fear: what can man do unto me?

It is better to trust in the Lord than to put confidence in man.

The Lord is my strength and my song, and is become my salvation.

The voice of rejoicing and salvation is in the tabernacles of the righteous: the right hand of the Lord doeth valiantly.

The right hand of the Lord is exalted: the right hand of the Lord doeth valiantly.

I shall not die but live, and declare the works of the Lord.

The Lord has chastened me sore: but he hath not given me over unto death.

Open to me the gates of righteousness: I will go into them, and I will praise Lord.

Theme: God Never Changes (a.k.a. "Jesus Christ is the same yesterday and today and tomorrow."—Hebrews 13:8)

1 Samuel 15:29

Psalm 100:5; 102:12, 25–2; 119:89

Malachi 3:6

Romans 11:29

James 1:12–18

Theme: The Power of the Tongue

Proverbs 6:12, 8:13, 17:4, 17:27–28, 31:26,

James 1:19, 3:1–12

Reflections

Epilogue:

Who Am I? I am His! We are His!

And His Truth Will Set Us Free!

> Behold, what manner of love the Father hath bestowed upon us, that
> we should be called the sons of God...
>
> 1 John 3:1

About a week before the manuscript was due, I found out that on top of everything else that had taken place over the last year-and-a-half, my father was going to have to have a *quadruple* bypass! The ensuing trip to Canada would also interfere with the time I was supposed to be spending making final revisions after the editing process!

I just couldn't believe it. As much as I love my dad, and feel for *his* plight, this would be about the *eighth* roadblock to this ministry. I was my father's only pillar of support. I didn't know if I had it in me to jump this last hurdle. Again, I prayed for peace, casting all of my cares on Him, and taking one day at a time. No matter what, I was going to finish this book and meet the deadline. But with everything coming to a head again over this critical time, how was I going to do it?

Of course, the Lord spoke to me one morning during a radio broadcast of *Turning Point,* hosted by Dr. David Jeremiah.[20] A wise Christian once told me that God will speak to us in our time of need, but we must be listening." I had just dropped my niece off at work. She had to go in a half-hour early that day for some reason (Hmmmm....). It was after I had left her that I tuned in to Dr. Jeremiah's 10 a.m. broadcast. And what do you know: he was addressing the issues of depression and anxiety! Glory to God, I *was listening.*

I found it very interesting, that the pastor opened his sermon with the following remark: "Before any great achievement, some measure of depression is usual."

Wow! That pretty much summed up the past eighteen months of my life. As mentioned at the beginning of the previous chapter, as soon as I signed the contract to write *3T Vision,* the bottom literally fell out. Trial after trial, tragedy after tragedy came against me, threatening to derail the project.

Consequently, I fought battle after battle against depression and anxiety, both tools of the devil. If I was going to triumph and complete God's work, I was going to have to continue to rely on the truth. And the Lord answered my plea in the broadcast of this sermon at the moment I needed it most. God is so good, and He's always on time!

Pastor Jeremiah continued with a powerful quotation from one of Charles Haddon Spurgeon's writings. Spurgeon (1835–1892), was a well-known preacher in England in the second half of the 19th century. At the same time that he was about to launch his largest ministry ever, he had *nagging doubts regarding his ability,* and ended up in a *deep depression.* Asking himself, "Who was I that I was to lead such a multitude?" Spurgeon finally concluded that "whenever the Lord is preparing a great blessing for a ministry, depression usually accompanies it."

This message mirrored the insecurities I felt when I signed my publishing contract, and then described the ensuing depression I experienced while writing. It had been an honor to be given an opportunity to write for the Lord! First of all, the Lord had given me the vision and the concept, and then Tate Publishing had picked up the project.

But of course the ink was barely dry on the contract when the turmoil began. As you already know, there were many times that I would beat myself up over feeling depressed, anxious and frustrated. "Who am I?" I would ask myself. Then it clicked! The song that I played at Camp JAM! The Holy Spirit had instructed me to play the song, "Who Am I," perhaps not only to touch the kids, but to tell me that *I am His!* As long as Satan can keep that "civil war" inside of us going, we're going to question our anointing, our ability to fulfill God's purpose for our lives. But what we all need to remember is that we are "children of the most high God" (1 John 3:1); we are "the apple of his eye" (Zechariah 2:8).

A great weight was suddenly lifted off my shoulders when Dr. Jeremiah confirmed that "depression is not a sin." Praise God! And then, to find out that David, one of the greatest kings of Israel, also battled the same evil forces! The following message gave me such peace.

The sermon was entitled, "David's Deep Depression, (Vol. 1)," and was based on 1 Samuel, Chapter 27. This particular chapter examines a period in David's life when he had an "enemy he could not master,"[21] and he was inundated by "expectations" and responsibility. Running from King Saul who sought to kill him, David was hiding in the mountains, in an "abode in wilderness in strongholds" (1 Samuel 23:14, KJV). In addition, he was responsible for 600 men and their families, and he knew that he was anointed to be King of Israel. The pressure was just too much. His depression deepened. He was exhausted and just about to give up. The King-to-Be, cried out to the Lord in moments of deep despair:

> Why standest thou afar off, O Lord? why hidest thou thyself in time of trouble?
>
> Psalms 10:1, KJV

> How long will thou forget me, O Lord? forever? How long wilt thou hide thy face from me?
>
> Psalms 13:1, KJV

And then, just as Christ cried out from the cross in order to fulfill the prophecy, David asked:

My, god, my God, why hast thou forsaken me? Why art thou so far
from helping me, and from the words of my roaring? (Psalms 22:1)

Getting back to Dr. Jeremiah's sermon, David had two choices.
He could flee and escape the pressure, or remember God's promises,
stand up to his enemy, and fulfill the expectations for his life. At
first, David fled. He went to live in the city of Gaph, in the land of
the Philistines! He actually retreated to the land of his enemy, the
homeland of Goliath!

But when we flee, says Jeremiah, we are left with a temporary, false
sense of security. What David didn't realize at the time, was that he
was now in more danger than ever. He was *sleeping with the enemy.*
The *enemy he could not master* was still out there; his *expectation* still
needed to be fulfilled. David defected and deceived God. But in the
end, God removed his enemy and David returned to Israel to fulfill
his destiny as King.

I felt such fellowship with David. I, too, felt like I was carrying the
weight of the world on my shoulders while trying to complete God's
assignment. Several family members were relying on me very heavily, all while I was trying to raise my son and write a book!

The effects of partial paralysis didn't help either. I was feeling (and
looking) increasingly exhausted.

Satan did not want this book written and read, and he was going
to challenge me until the very end!

During his sermon, Dr. Jeremiah reminded me of two things.
First of all, like David, I was "wrestling not against flesh and
blood, but against principalities, against powers, against the rul-
ers of the darkness of this world, against spiritual wickedness in
high places" (Ephesians 6:12). Secondly, I "needed to hang on to
the promises of God instead of drowning in depression."[22] (Jeremiah, *Turning Point*).

The scripture that immediately came to mind was, "I will not
leave you, nor forsake you" (Joshua 1:5b, NIV). I began to meditate on
that scripture, determined to find peace. *My Father would never leave
me nor forsake me.* I had to *master my enemy* by refusing to give in to
Satan's pressure, and *fulfill God's expectation* for my writing ministry.

Again, I had to put on the whole armor of God (Ephesians 6:10–17), fulfill the vision, and triumph over tragedy once again.

It is just several days before I submit the *3T Vision* manuscript, and I am waiting to hear from my dad as to the date of his surgery. So I will "take no thought for the morrow; for the morrow shall take thought for the things of itself" (Matthew 6:34). Continuing to feed my soul with the truth, I will pray, believe, and breathe; knowing that God's truth remains the same yesterday, today and forever.

On more than one occasion during the storms of the past eighteen months, the Lord spoke three simple words to me: "Trust in me," He said, revealing that life's turbulent circumstances are not for *me* to *figure out;* they are *for Him* to *look after.* In so doing, I can share that seed with you: while He is looking after the stuff meant to distract us, we can be busy fulfilling his calling on our lives.

Whether the Lord whispers His calling into your ear, or sends an angelic messenger (as He did that day in my hospital room), stay focused on your vision with 3T Vision. Don't give up, and don't give in, because *truth always triumphs over tragedy.*

May God bless you and keep you in His infinite care. And may He continue the good work in you, carrying you through to *your vision's* full completion (Philippians 1:6).

Endnotes

1. Meyer, Joyce. Battle Field of the Mind Devotional, 5-6.

2. Moore, Beth. *Praying God's Word*, 38.

3. Meyer, Joyce. Battlefield of the Mind, 185.

4. Austin, Karen. Blind Trust, 88.

5. Dickow, Gregory. Chicago: Changing Your Life. TBN television broadcast.

6. Austin, 105.

7. Austin, 106.

8. Reprinted by permission, Austin, 180-182.

9. Austin, 208.

10. Austin, 213.

11. Nediva. www.houseofruththomaston.org

12. Osteen, Pastor Joel. Your Best Life Now, 251.

13. Osteen, 24.

14. Meyer, 45.

15. Huch, Pastor Larry. New Life Christian Center. TBN Broadcast, Dec. 4, 2005.

16. Osteen, 79.

17. Osteen, 34-35.

18. Dotson, Emily. Sid Roth's Messianic Vision, 2003.

19   Hall, Mark. "Who Am I," Copyright 2003. Club Zone Music/ SWECS Music. All rights reserved. Used by permission.

20. Jeremiah, Pastor Dr. David. Turning Point: "David's Deep Depression (Vol. 1)." Radio broadcast, Immanuel Broadcasting Network, Cartersville, GA, Sept. 21, 2006.

21. Jeremiah, "David's Deep Depression (Vol. 1)"

22. Jeremiah, "David's Deep Depression (Vol. 1)"

Bibliography

Austin, Karen. *Blind Trust: a child's legacy.* Crossroads Counseling: 1301 Shiloh Rd., Suite 610, Kennesaw, GA 30144.

Dickow, Pastor Gregory. TBN television broadcast. Chicago: *Changing Your Life.*

Dotson, Emily. *Use God's Word as Your Healing Foundation, or You Will Take on Deception.* Sid Roth's Messianic Visions www.sidroth. org/healing_main15.htm, 2003.

Hall, Mark. *Who Am I.* Club Zone Music/SWECS Music, Copyright 2003. All Rights Reserved. Used By Permission.

Huch, Pastor Larry. TBN television broadcast. New Beginnings Christian Center: Portland Oregon. December 4, 2005.

Jeremiah, Dr. David. *Lifetouch Ministries:* El Cajon, California. "David's Deep Depression (Vol.1)." Radio broadcast, IBN, Cartersville, GA, September 21, 2006.

Long, Bishop Eddie. *Praise the Lord.* California: TBN television broadcast. January 25, 2006.

Meyer, Joyce. *Battlefield of the Mind: Winning the Battle in Your Mind.* New York: Warner Faith (Time Warner Book Group), 1995.

Meyer, Joyce. *Battlefield of the Mind: Devotional.* New York: Warner Faith (Time Warner Book Group), 2005.

Moore, Beth. *Praying God's Word: Breaking Free from Spiritual Strongholds.* Nashville: Broadman and Holman Publishers, 2000.

Nediva. www.houseofruththomaston.org.

Olsteen, Pastor Joel. *Your Best Life Now: 7 Steps to Living Life at Your Full Potential.* New York: Warner Faith (Time Warner Book Group), 2004.

WebMD.com. *www.webmd.com/hw/depression*

Wilkinson, Bruce. *The Prayer of Jabez.* Sisters, OR: Multnomah Publishers, 1999.